W9-CNP-413

Give me your tired, your poor,
Your huddled masses yearning to breathe free,
The wretched refuse of your teeming shore.

Famous lines *often associated with the Statue of Liberty are from "The New Colossus", a sonnet by American poet Emma Lazarus (1849–1887).*

BUILDING AMERICA

Immigrant Stories of Hope and Hardship

by

Many Who Love This Country and the Freedom for Which It Stands

First Edition Publication

The Ardent Writer Press
Brownsboro, Alabama

Visit the Building America Page at
www.ArdentWriterPress.com

For general information about publishing with The Ardent Writer Press contact *steve@ardentwriterpress.com* or forward mail to:
The Ardent Writer Press,
Box 25
Brownsboro, Alabama 35741.

This is a first edition of a collection of stories and poems entitled *Building America: Immigrant Stories of Hope and Hardship*. All rights reserved by the authors. Excerpts of text may be posted online only for a noncommercial use, provided quotations do not exceed a total of over three hundred (300) words.

Cover composition by Steve Gierhart, The Ardent Writer Press, using Photoshop techniques. Photo of the Statue of Liberty for the cover and title page as well as the photo of immigrants being sworn in as US citizens at the Grand Canyon (Prologue) from Flickr with attribution to Creative Commons' 2.0 Generic (CC BY 2.0). Profile images on cover from Deposit Photos and PxHere. Photos in the interior were provided by the respective authors.

Library of Congress Cataloging-in-Publication Data

Building America: Immigrant Stories of Hope and Hardship

p. cm. (Ardent Writer Press) ISBN 978-1-64066-104-2 (paperback-black and white); 978-1-64066-105-9 (hardcover-color); eBook mobi Kindle version ISBN 978-1-64066-106-6

Library of Congress Control Number 2019945732

Library of Congress and BISAC Suggested Subject Headings
- Immigrants.
- Memoir.
- Immigrants--United States--History--Case studies.
- Immigrants--United States--Interviews.
- Immigrants--United States--Social conditions.

BISAC Subject Headings
- SOC007000   SOCIAL SCIENCE / Emigration & Immigration
- BIO002000   BIOGRAPHY & AUTOBIOGRAPHY / Cultural, Ethnic & Regional / General
- BIO026000   BIOGRAPHY & AUTOBIOGRAPHY / Personal Memoirs

First Edition (Various Authors with © Original Copyright 2020)

TABLE OF CONTENTS – BUILDING OF AMERICA

STORIES

BUILDING AMERICA

Acknowledgments

by Mary Saad Assel and Glenn O'Kray

IN HOPE THAT OUR COUNTRY continues to thrive upon the shoulders of newcomers, we would like to express our sincere gratitude to our spouses — Jane O'Kray and Ernie Assel — for their on-going support in our gathering stories and encouraging us to put this book together. Many thanks to our editor Kate Robinson and our supportive friends and colleagues, Nancy Owen Nelson, and Ed and Martha Demerly. We would also like to extend our gratitude to our friend — Pastor Sel Harris who strongly applauded our mission and showed great interest in the book. This book would not have been possible without our outstanding authors. We owe them an enormous debt of gratitude for sharing their stories and their willingness to join us in dedicating all royalties to the American Civil Liberties Union. In particular, we would like to thank one of our authors and publisher Steve Gierhart for his generous contributions, talent, and expertise in the art of publication.

On Thursday, September 23, 2010 *Grand Canyon National Park in coordination with The Department of Homeland Security hosted a naturalization ceremony at the Mather Amphitheater on the South Rim. This was the first time in history that Grand Canyon National Park hosted such an event.*

Under blue skies and before a breathtaking view, 23 individuals from 12 different countries including, Colombia, Dominican Republic, Guatemala, Japan, Mexico, Morocco, Australia, Trinidad and Tobago, Uruguay, Venezuela, Vietnam and Zambia, became naturalized citizens. Park employees and visitors watched on as the candidates stated the Oath of Allegiance, and received their certificates of naturalization.

John M. Ramirez, Acting District Director for the US Citizenship and Immigration Services (USCIS) administered the Oath of Allegiance.

A keynote address was given by USCIS Ombudsman January Contreras. Ms. Contreras stated, "Everyday, we welcome new and diverse stories and heritages into the great patchwork of our Nation. United by our devotion to the Constitution and to the civic engagement it inspires, Americans remain committed to the fundamental principles established over two hundred years ago."

(NPS Photo-Michael Quinn from Flicker/Creative Commons)

Prologue

by Mary Saad Assel and Glenn O'Kray

THIS BOOK IS ABOUT IMMIGRANTS who came to this country to search for a better life. Whether they came to America as settlers or immigrants, their accomplishments have become an integral part of the fabric of this country. They lead us through their journey of hardships and embrace us through their successes and failures. They no longer dream of freedom but are witnesses unto the nations beyond our borders to the definition of freedom. They demonstrate the importance of living among energetic, unyielding people and have made this country more colorful and appealing. They are the living miracles that made America what it is today.

Miracles do not hide behind closed doors nor do they roam the skies to come to our rescue at will. However, when desire and need are intertwined with passion and personal drive, we learn to create our own miracles.

Millions of people around the world live in turmoil. They focus on conquering their fears of famine and oppression. They endure political unrest and are at times held hostage to war and conflict in their own countries. When opportunities arise and they find the means and courage to leave their countries, many make America their target destination. America is proclaimed to respect people's rights and to give them more independence and freedom than any other country. Desperate immigrants leave their nation of birth to become fearless hunters in the "world of the free." To them, America is the mother of hope and the goddess of hospitality. She is known to spread her wide wings around the shoulders of newcomers and offer them confidence and security. No sooner than they arrive in America, word of mouth finds its way across the oceans to inform kin and relatives of America's open heart and tangible treasures. They invite their loved ones to join them. Over time, a father becomes a grandfather, great-grandfather, and great, great, great, grandfather to generations of immigrants who have settled in the arms of their new mother—America.

The discovery of the American continent in 1492 led Caucasian explorers to circumnavigate the globe and begin the conquest of the Americas. The era of slavery and colonization began by the mid-sixteenth century and the flooding of bullion into Europe had a powerful impact on the economy of the world. It takes will, desperation, wit, and brainpower for a country to grow and expand as quickly as America. From the onset, it was an expansive, fertile land shared by English settlers and natives. Over time, world powers fought to claim it but eventually gave in to England. Frustrated English settlers became soldiers and fought against the oppression of King George III. Once the colonies gained their independence in 1776, American laws and governments were set in place.

Shortly after, America became the envy of world powers and the land of opportunity. Immigrants were no longer immigrants but rather fathers and founders of a land hungry for lucrative industries and exquisite architecture. From east to west, small farms turned into large cities, trails became railroads, and small businesses were converted to shopping malls—all by the willful labor of immigrants. Following the eighteenth-century industrial revolution and the twentieth-century automotive and assembly line, America expanded in wealth and prosperity.

Historically, it wasn't unusual for immigrants to be turned away, but immigration officials did not physically or psychologically abuse them. Today's recent surge in immigration and increase in anti-Semitic and anti-Muslim rhetoric have led to internal acts of terrorism and countless mass shootings. America, a country once perceived as the welcoming "Mother" of immigrants had become the cage that imprisoned them and their children. Safety and security were replaced with hate and unrest. America is no longer the world's envy—neither does it want to be. Patriotism has been replaced by nationalism and hatred. America has essentially locked its doors to immigration.

According to Maslow's hierarchy, once we are fed and rested, our second most important need is safety. How is it possible for immigrants to feel safe if there's a chance that some disturbed individual or terrorist barges into a place of work, worship, or entertainment, and takes their lives because he felt hatred toward the "other" or those whose physical appearances or faith differs from their own? Sadly, over time, victims' stories become part of the fabric of everyone's story, a theme that makes us wonder if hate crimes will ever be eradicated. On a more fundamental level, most studies reveal they cannot. But they can be reduced through education, communication, and improved community relations.

The issue with hate crimes, mass shootings, and other forms of violence has led researchers to investigate the causes and origins of hate. One of the most important findings was the lack of education about the "other." For example, a study by the Public Research Institute reveals that more than six in ten of those who kill, or abuse Muslims have never had a conversation with a Muslim. Psychologist Gordon Allport concludes in his seminal book *The Nature of Prejudice* that meaningful contact with those who are different is crucial in reducing prejudice. Hence, when facing this epidemic of unprecedented hate crimes, it is crucial for people to interact with one another. There needs to be a humane connectedness between the hater and the potential victim. Reports by the Century Foundation Institute have shown that increased knowledge about the "other" can lower levels of discomfort and reduce the number of crimes. Victims who are targeted because of their race, religion, sexual orientation, or ethnicity would feel less vulnerable if they could easily communicate with racists and show them that they are human like everyone else.

Today, people from all over the country are rising to fight hate and to re-normalize America's doors to legal immigration. It is very important for community centers and college campuses to raise awareness of hate crimes. Community education through campus groups can make a difference in how students perceive each other and how some raise awareness to the injustice of hate crimes. Influencing policy at the federal and state level will inspire early intervention to reduce hate and violence. Perhaps historical and epistemological dynamics will broaden our understanding of the underlying causes of hate and prejudice, but for the moment this is where we are. We need to keep our minds open to immigrants and return to who we were prior to the rise of white nationalism. Hate should be eliminated.

Much more can be learned from future studies that link offenders' perceptions and beliefs about the groups they target, and a comprehensive analysis of the commonalities and differences can shed light on hate crime strands and variations. The different levels of prejudice toward immigrants can be dealt with and prevention strategies can be implemented. It is the responsibility of every learned person to act and to speak up. Conversations about diversity are crucial. People have human rights and when those rights are violated, educators, students, politicians, community leaders, and social institutions need to take the lead and put an end to ignorance. They need to raise awareness of the "other" to reduce or even end hate crimes and violence. Without them, America would not exist. We cannot unravel all the nuances and complexities that encompass white nationalism nor can we capture the zeitgeist of earlier centuries, but we can offer a powerful and distinctive solution. If we cannot learn to accept one another, we can learn to build tolerance.

Mary Assel *(below) and* **Glenn O'Kray** *(above) are the project leads for* Building America: Immigrant Stories of Hope and Hardship. *They coordinate all group activities and compiled the collection. They are also responsible for initiating and promoting the project's goals of humanizing immigrants in America and for setting up the project's links to the American Civil Liberties Union (ACLU). All proceeds from the project and contributors will be given to the ACLU for their use in protecting the rights of the world's citizens in the United States.*

Martha Christensen Demerly *is a proud native of South Dakota Irish and Danish immigrants who pioneered there before the territory attained statehood. A retired high school English teacher who earned a Master of Theology at age 74, Martha enjoys leading bible study classes and being the matriarch of a large and thriving family – all South Dakota wannabees. Established by immigrants, South Dakota's greatest export is its people.*

Her poem is reflection of her great paternal grandfather, Leopold Hansen, and great-great maternal grand father, Jesse Jessen. The photos are of Leopold Hansen, who emigrated from Denmark and arrived alone in Dakota Territory at age seventeen; the photo above shows him as a prosperous farmer along the Missouri River near Vermillion, South Dakota.

To Dave, Mary and all! Thank you for welcoming me as part of you. Love. Martha

There Was a Young Dane went Forth

There was a young Dane went forth,
    leaving his home, his village, his country,
    and all that he left and all that he met
    became part of him for his own life, for that of his children,
    and for many generations to come.

The sea voyage became part of this Dane,
    the landing at Boston, the immigration delays,
    the goodhearted people of the missionary societies,
    his fellow and equally confused emigres,
    all became part of him.

The journey across a new land –
    through Philadelphia, Chicago –
    with fellow travelers
    speaking varied tongues but sharing common expectancies,
    all these became part of him.

The prospect of owning,
    of growing rich in land, or produce or goods,
    the promise of building legacies,
    all became part of him.

And the quiet daughter of the violin teacher's family,
    she who spoke several languages,
    who wore embroidered bodices,
    who sang the old songs trillingly,
    who loved the flowers of the fields and all small creatures,
    she became part of him.

1

H. BUTLER. Vermillion. D. T

So that they wedded and loved
    and brought forth sons and daughters.
And then, schools and books and ambitious dreams
        became part of them
        as the great happiness of building a home filled their lives:
            with the cooing and shushing of the mother at work,
            and the stern commands of the father at his work,
            with the laughter of children at their games,
            and the serious repeated recitation of schoolhouse
                    lessons,
            with the tedious chores of childhood –
                    always assigned and sometimes neglected –
            with the constant and satisfying labor of homemaking
                    and homebuilding,
        all became part of them.

And hardships became part of them—
            the taxing sorrows of sickness and hard times,
            the paternal worry for sons gone off to war,
            the lasting loss of beloved family—
            all these became part of them.

And triumphs to hallmark their lives became part of them—
            graduations and marriages,
            honors bestowed upon their children,
            and the rewards of long life—
                    memory, devotion, pride —
            all became part of them.

And all that became part of them became part of me...

Martha Christensen Demerly
(Modeled after Walt Whitman's "There was a Child
went Forth")

This is Mike "Miklos" Adler *in June of 1953 after being drafted and doing a tour of Korea with the US Army. He said after "staying in concentration camps (during WWII), Korea was a picnic." Mike lives with his wife, Rita, in Redford, Michigan. He spends his time planting flowers and vegetables.*

Mike "Miklos" Adler

I WAS BORN in an agricultural area of Hungary in 1930. My family was middle class. My father owned a small broom factory, employing four workers as well as my mom. As a youth, I was involved in many sports, especially soccer. I completed my eighth grade when the Germans walked into my country. There had been no resistance.

The Germans took away the business licenses of Jews, thereby depriving my father of his livelihood. Jews were put into a ghetto, then we were transferred for a short time to a big farm. There was not much to eat, but I was able to sneak out and get food from neighboring farms. I might have escaped, but I knew that if I had done so, my family would have been killed in retribution.

We were transferred onto a train with no food or toilet facilities to Birkenau. The trip took three days. My mother, father, my seven-year-old brother and I reached the camp, but the notorious camp physician, Josef Mengele, known as "the Angel of Death," pulled me by the collar and directed me into a separate line. I never again saw my family. I then went to Auschwitz where I was tattooed.

I was transferred to Buna where I worked at a German chemical factory owned by I. G. Farben. It looked like the Ford Rouge plant in Dearborn, Michigan except that an electrical fence surrounded the facility. There were lots of Polish Jews there. I was one of the few Hungarian Jews, so I didn't speak the same language as most of the prisoners. A nineteen-year-old befriended me. He became my protector. We would have a piece of bread for breakfast and then soup for lunch and dinner. Our barracks had no toilet facilities; we had to use outhouses. By the outhouses there was a storage building filled with clothing and other items taken from the prisoners. I was able to sneak clothing out so that I might trade it for bread and butter with Polish civilians who worked there.

Jews wore yellow triangles on their clothing; German felons wore green triangles. The work was hard. Many did not survive the first week. We had to walk from the camp to the Farben workplace.

Rita and Mike *on a vacation to Las Vegas in June 1999.*

We were forced to walk some 25 miles from Buna to Gliwitz. Many did not make it. Then, we were put on a train with no roof, which took us to Dora, near Nordhausen. Of some 3000–4000, maybe 1000 survived. There were stacks of dead bodies. We survivors worked in a facility under a mountain, an underground factory, on V1 and V2 missiles. I carried bomb components from one assembly line to another. Anyone who was caught trying to sabotage production was hanged. There were two or three hangings every day.

I was always optimistic and believed that, somehow, I would survive that ordeal. I would steal food thinking that I would rather be killed than starve to death. When American and British bombers flew overhead, I tried to run into a bunker, but a German officer said that no Jews were allowed. Shortly thereafter, a bomb hit that same bunker and killed those Germans.

I had another protector, a Polish political prisoner. He would give me extra food. We were sent in another topless train car to Bergen-Belsen. There were sugar beets in the surrounding fields. I found a sewer, followed it and sneaked out of the camp. I came upon American soldiers. They could tell we were prisoners by our clothes. They gave us corned beef and pickles which made us sick. British soldiers took us to a refugee camp.

I ultimately went to a trade school while I worked for an American Jewish relief organization. I learned how to repair cars and trucks and eventually was the assistant transportation officer, keeping 50-60 trucks operating. I played on a Jewish soccer team in Germany. I was ready to go to Israel, but a friend convinced me to go to America. I came to the US alone by ship. There was a major storm during our transit, and we all got sick.

I arrived in New York and was walking the streets when I heard someone call out, "Hey, Mickey!" It was the girlfriend of a soccer friend I had. She helped me get settled. I got a job delivering food to delicatessens and food carts. I had to get up at 3 a.m. to begin my day. I was paid $40 per week and got a free lunch. I learned English by going to the movies and watching three shows per day. I developed a side hustle in the ping pong and pool halls.

I got a job as a mechanic and began making $80 per week. Another soccer friend of mine convinced me to go to Detroit. I belonged to a semi-professional soccer team. I took a job in Detroit working for Dexter Chevrolet.

I was drafted in 1952 and went to Korea. I was sent to communication school and assigned to the battalion headquarters. There were eight-inch guns that went off every few minutes, making sleep impossible. After staying in concentration camps, Korea was a picnic. I stayed there for a while after the war. I even became an American citizen while in an Eastern country!

I returned to Detroit and worked again as a mechanic. Another fellow and I set up a partnership fixing cars in Southfield, just outside of Detroit. We found that the customers we had had at the Chevy dealerships followed us.

I married and stayed in the difficult relationship for 30 years, until I divorced. Then I started a used-car dealership with a friend who was an Israeli-Arab Christian. We prospered.

Ultimately, I remarried, to Rita, a wonderful woman. We have been married for 26 years. We adopted a wonderful daughter, Cheyenne, who is now 22 years old.

I have returned to Hungary twice, once in 2002 and again in 2018. I hardly knew my hometown, and only recognized it because of the Catholic church and the Corona Hotel.

I love America, where there is more freedom than anywhere else on Earth.

Rita Adler

MY PARENTS WERE MARRIED in an air raid shelter during World War II. I was born on a small island, Gozo, which is a part of Malta. My father came to the United States first. He was unskilled, and in our homeland, he had no ability to make a decent living. In Malta only a few went to college.

My dad came to New York. He would come back to Malta every year, just long enough to get my mother pregnant. She had three kids who died. My mother's tragic life was magnified by her father's and brother's having been shipwrecked and dying. I almost died as well. My mother had no sense of smell and on one occasion fed me kerosene. I lost my hair and would have to have my stomach pumped frequently.

My mother, brother, sister and I came to the United States when I was five years old. I had rarely seen my dad, so I was anxious to see him. We moved to Corktown in Detroit which included a great number of Irish and Maltese. My dad was really into sports. In fact, he died at Tiger Stadium. I attended Most Holy Trinity Catholic Grade School and then Crestwood High School.

I received an associate degree in nursing from Henry Ford Community College and continued my education at Wayne State University. I worked at Wyandotte Hospital and St. John's Providence Hospital. I served in the emergency room and in the oncology unit. I loved my job. Unfortunately, I had to retire early as I had four different types of cancer. I was one of ten people in the world identified with one of the forms of cancer. My immunity was so compromised by radiation and chemotherapy that I could not continue working in a hospital environment.

I have a wonderful son, Sergio Mautone. He is a graphics artist and actor. I returned to Malta five times, but I have no memory of having lived there. There are plusses and minuses to life in Malta. Health care is much cheaper there. I had a dental problem there which cost me $300. In the United States it would have cost $3,000. However, if you were severely ill, it was necessary to go to Italy as you might not have survived in Malta. There are two extremes in Malta. Either you are dirt poor or very rich. On the other hand, I miss the social aspect of Malta. Nobody locks their door there. People have a better quality of life there.

Rita was very happy *in her nursing career. She graduated in 1984 and is seen here getting her associates degree in nursing. Like her husband, Mike, she is retired and loves gardening, both for flowers and vegetables.*

Mary Assel *is a Dearborn native and the daughter of Lebanese immigrants. She worked at Henry Ford College from 1999 – 2012. She was an instructor, advisor, and director of the English Language Institute. In her retirement, Mary spends most of her time writing and traveling with her husband Ernie, her children and grandchildren. She has authored two books, published and presented on domestic violence, second language acquisition, brain, memory, and retention, Arab women and culture, religious barriers, and interfaith.*

The photo above is of Mary's grandfather, Mislim Hadous (left) and his friend Kamal Bazzi (right) from the early 1900s.

Mary Saad Assel

AFTER RETIREMENT from Henry Ford College in Dearborn, Michigan and the passing of my father in 2012, I spent six years watching over my mother. My mother was legally blind and took advantage of my presence to talk to me about my grandparents, specifically my grandfather, whose stories are now embedded in my long-term memory. For the sake of truths behind immigrant stories, I rejoice in being a descendant of Mislim Hadous, a man for whom I extend the utmost respect.

Mislim immigrated from his country, Syria—later partitioned into Greater Lebanon— in 1904 to evade religious tension and conflict while under the rule of the Ottoman Empire. The Turkish state controlled much of Southeast Europe, Western Asia and North Africa between the fourteenth and early twentieth centuries. The empire declined at the end of World War I in 1918, but Mislim was already freed from religious or political persecution when he immigrated to America, the land of opportunity, 14 years earlier. His story resonates with most American immigrants who made the attempt to attain freedom and take control of their own lives. According to the New York bound ship's passenger arrival records, he landed on Ellis Island along with a few other Syrian friends and relatives to begin his new life.

Mislim worked as a peddler in Manhattan for two consecutive years. He purchased a pushcart to sell fruits, vegetables, and fish. He roomed with friends but his unabashed focus on improving his economic well-being was an evocation of the successes of many of immigrants before him.

With hope to improve his financial status, he moved to Michigan City, Indiana in 1910 to work at the Michigan Central Railroad. He remained at the railroad until the close of World War I. The job was less yielding than he had anticipated, and tired of moving tons of earth in wheelbarrows and on the backs of mules, he moved to Highland Park, Michigan in 1915.

He worked at Ford Motor Company's Highland Park Plant and was paid $5.00 a day, double the existing factory pay rate at the time. Eventually bored with the monotony of the assembly line, he applied for a transfer to the Dearborn Ford Rouge Plant in 1928 to work in the cafeteria. By then, he had saved enough money to purchase a home in Dearborn, located within walking distance from the plant.

He married Fatima and raised four children, my mother Zihra being the youngest. Mislim's American dream was interrupted by the Great Depression of 1929. Known for her strong will and take-charge personality, a trait that both my mother and I inherited, Fatima never sugar-coated anything. She gave her honest opinion and told the painful truth rather than make anyone feel better with a lie. She told my grandfather, "Don't worry about the Depression. I'll handle this"—and she did. She turned her home into a Bed and Breakfast. She saved every penny and added a handsome sum to the little my grandfather had accumulated over the years.

In 1933, they returned to Lebanon to wait out the Depression and feed off the land that Mislim had inherited from his parents. Unfortunately, he passed away several years later, making it difficult for Fatima to support her family alone.

By 1947, shortly after Lebanon had received its independence from France, she urged her children to return to America to re-establish their lives. My uncles Charlie and Mohamed had returned in 1946. They resettled in Michigan, found work, rented a home, and awaited the arrival of their families.

My mother had married my father Mahmoud, a Lebanese national. Accompanied by her brother's wife and two children, she embarked on her journey to America. With no more than the clothing on her back and a pair of open sandals, she landed in New York in December of 1947. Shivering, she stared at the Statue of Liberty's sandals and wondered if she too, was clueless of America's cruel and cold winters. My uncle, who awaited her arrival, covered her with a blanket and teasingly said, "Welcome to America!"

My father joined my mom the following year. Together, they started a family with hope of living the American dream. Dad worked at the railroad for a few months, then took a job at the Ford Motor Company Rouge Plant's assembly line.

In an elusive search for improvement, a notion that was at the heart of his dream, he left the assembly line in 1952 and opened a convenience store on Mack Avenue in Detroit. My parents worked hand in hand. With Mom's innate business skills and Dad's hard-working hands the business was prosperous. They hired a housekeeper to watch over us while they worked and invested in real estate.

By 1961, they decided to return to Lebanon, a decision they lived to regret. Once they realized that economic opportunities were paramount in America more than any other country, they returned to Michigan in 1965. Mom worked as a butcher at the Dearborn Sausage Company while Dad searched for a business. They worked hard to reestablish their lives in Michigan. It was their repeated sacrifices that gave their children and future generations ample opportunity to learn that hard work is always rewarded. Their lives were richer, better, and more complete. Their dreams underlined a life that carried the worthy end of liberty and self-determination.

Today, as I think of Mislim and his assortment of aspirations and accomplishments, I admire all immigrants who pursue their dreams. His dream was to return to his country with some tangible wealth and he did. His Model T accompanied him on his journey back to Lebanon. He drove it with pride through the bumpy, stone-paved roads of his village to demonstrate to friends and family that there was nothing like living the American dream. Grandma's trunks were filled with ready-to-wear clothing, household appliances, coal-irons, radios, pillows, sheets, and more. America had given them the opportunity to grow and flourish socially and economically. My mother was proud to be the daughter of Fatima and Mislim and to be an American. She explained that dreams are intangible, but no less intangible than the realities that lie in the mysteries of our futures.

Whether engaged in a low-paying job or highly skilled occupation, America is filled with vibrant and energetic people who come from all over the globe. Our dreams are embedded in the Bill of Rights that are handed down from generation to generation as was Mislim's dream that was handed to my mother, then to me, my children, and my grandchildren.

Sam Baydoun

MY STORY TRULY STARTS in 1905, when a young man from Bint Jbeil in southern Lebanon set a course for a new life in the States. After his arrival in Ellis Island with $12 in his pocket, he traveled to Michigan City, Indiana, to look for work around the only countrymen he knew there, working day in and day out on a railroad. Years later, he finally settled down in Dearborn, Michigan, and made a living at the Ford Rouge plant. This man is my grandfather, Hajj Aly Baydoun, and he single handedly planted the seeds for my family to pursue the American Dream.

I also grew up in Bint Jbeil, but my family fled in 1978 when the civil war was raging throughout the country. I was 15 years old and came here with my parents, five of my seven brothers, and one sister. We joined two brothers who were living in Dearborn, Michigan; it was my oldest brother Gary who petitioned for us to come to the United States. We flew from Beirut to Amman, Jordan and then New York to Detroit. My dad worked for the water department in Bint Jbeil, but in the US, it was my two brothers who supported the family until we all got on our feet. We all came here searching for a better life with nothing but blind faith and a resolve to succeed.

When I arrived, I did not speak a word of English, and I even got lost on the way to school. It was my first day, and luckily, a concerned man approached me, to which my only reply was "Fordson." He pointed me in the right direction, which, in hindsight, I also take figuratively. Education was the only sure thing I knew.

French was my second language in Lebanon, and I became nearly fluent in English within six months. I also adapted to American culture readily, fascinated by sports stars like Magic Johnson, Kareem Abdul Jabbar, and Julius Erving, and stayed glued to our television when Three's Company, The Jefferson's, or Welcome Back, Kotter were on.

I got my associate degree from Henry Ford Community College in 1984; I am still friends with some of my former classmates, going so far as to arrange a reunion with them and our English instructor, Ed Demerly, in 2019. In 1986, I earned my bachelor's degree from the

Sam Baydoun *is a husband, father, and a dedicated public servant. He's been a real estate broker for the past 34 years, helping families realize the American dream of being homeowners. In 2018, Sam Baydoun made history by being elected the first Arab American Wayne County Commissioner for his district.*

Detroit College of Business, now known as Davenport University. That same year, I got my realtor's license, not knowing that it would be one of my life's calling for years to come. Not even in my wildest dreams did I think

I would find such a passion for the real estate business and make any sort of name for myself. I stand now with an estimated $400 million in sales and listed as a top 10 producer for Century 21 in the State of Michigan.

I married Ibtihal in 1989, and she was actually the biggest driving force of my real estate career. She had a major health crisis in 2016, and I have provided her with home care since. I have two daughters, Lily and Angela. Lily is in her first year of high school. Angela is a student at the University of Michigan. My sons, Ali and Mohammad, are in the real estate business with me.

I have always felt that there is no greater calling than public service. In 2018, I decided to give back to the community that shaped me into the man I am today by running for public office. I was unable to divert focus from my family and run for City Council the year prior, so the sudden availability of a Wayne County Commission seat felt like it was my fated time. I had widespread support throughout my city due in large part to my involvement in community matters and building both personal and business relationships through real estate. The commissioner vacating the seat, Gary Woronchak, endorsed me, the mayor of Dearborn supported me, and former Congressman John Dingell, Congresswoman Debbie Dingell, and several other high-profile political figures were in my camp. However, the most important figure linked to my campaign was my daughter Lily; her star power secured us the win.

I believe that the United States is the greatest country on this planet. It is the land of opportunities. It gave me the opportunity to succeed and start a beautiful family in a safe environment. This country provides security and education. I am very grateful for what this country provided me.

Susan Bercea *is a nurse, mother and recently a new grandmother who lives in Dearborn, Michigan. She enjoys gardening, reading and cooking traditional Romanian food.*

The photo is of Susan in her native country of Romania in the late 1960s.

Susan Bercea

I WAS THE THIRD CHILD OF EIGHT born in a small rural village called Cublesul-Somesan in 1952 Communist Romania. My family was quite poor. Village life was one of hard work. However, my parents loved each other and loved us well. Growing up I thought we were the wealthiest people in the world because we had a happy childhood.

We sustained ourselves by working the family farm. We grew grains and made sunflower oil. We raised all kinds of animals including: pigs, cows, sheep, goats, turkeys, ducks and even had a donkey! We churned butter and made cheese. We had a loom and made our own clothing, linens and rugs. In sharing stories of my childhood, my children often exclaimed that how we lived was like the 1800s reflected by the television program, *Little House on the Prairie*! There were no nursing homes for the elderly or facilities for those who were handicapped. Everybody took care of each other in the village.

My father was a dedicated Christian man. Because he was one of the few villagers who could read, he hosted an "underground" church in our home to read the Bible and pray together. Orthodox believers could openly worship in those times. However, my family was Protestant. He was frequently taken from the family by the "Securitate" (Romanian Communist Police), put in jail, and often beaten. My dad never complained. He took this on as his cross. Even after his death, the police would come to our home to question my mother. It was difficult for Communists to understand how educated people could be people of faith.

Because of our beliefs, my siblings and I were frequently ridiculed in school. Schoolchildren were strongly encouraged to become "Pioneers." That was a Communist youth organization. One day my oldest sister came home with a red scarf, the symbol of that organization. My dad was not pleased, to say the least. He took her aside and had a talk about our values and why she could not join.

My beloved father passed away suddenly in the fall of 1965. This was a great loss for our family since he was a noble man. But my mother was a strong woman and carried on. Because we were good students, two of my siblings and I went to boarding school, beginning at the age of 8, 10 and 12. The school was very far from our village in a town called Abrud, which was tucked away in a beautiful forest of the Apuseni Mountains. I would go back home in the summers to help my mom in the countryside.

Before America

My husband John and I met at the church we both attended in the large city of Cluj during my time as a young student in my early 20s. He also came from a large family with 10 siblings. They were wealthy and had lots of land, but it had been seized by the government. Before his beloved mother Ana passed, a prayerful woman of God, he promised her to help take care of the family. He had the dream of a better life in America in his heart. He made a plan to flee to America soon after. Spies in the church notified the police of his plans, and he was caught, beaten and jailed. He got sick in jail, and after six difficult months he was released. Fortunately, the president gave him amnesty. He fulfilled his dream when he made it to America legally with several siblings in the spring of 1980.

During this time, I had finished nursing school and was helping to support my widowed mother and siblings. John and I kept in touch and made the decision to marry. When he came back to visit Romania in the spring of

1984, we were engaged and had a civil ceremony. The following year I prepared to join him in America.

♁ ❀ ♁

In America

In May 1985, I got on a plane and left my home country behind for a new land. I made the journey to the USA and before landing in New York, I was deep in thought while flying. I was overcome with many emotions about what my new life would be like in this new country. I quietly prayed, asking the Lord to help me do my part, believing that He is faithful and will do His part. I wanted and was ready to embrace the best that America represented.

We got married in a small Romanian immigrant church in Detroit, Michigan that July. We started our life and had three children in rapid succession. I had taken "British English" in school and needed to learn the American style of speaking and idioms. I attended Detroit's International Institute. I had expected the education to be more academic and rigorous. However, I learned conversational English, which was just what I needed. I was fortunate to make a friend who served as my "culture mentor." She taught me the basics of living in America—what to eat at breakfast, lunch and dinner, introduced me to American banking, and took me to the historic buildings and landmarks in Detroit. It was kind of her to help me learn the new culture.

My mother came from Romania to visit us while I was pregnant with my third child. It was her first time on a plane. During her visit, John became suddenly ill and was diagnosed with late stage cancer. The prognosis was poor and in three short months he passed away in June of 1990. Fortunately, my mom was still with us and was willing, being a widow herself, to stay and help me raise my children. She was a wonderful "bunica" (grandmother) to Priscila, Jonathan and Emanuela (Ema).

With three small children under three years of age, those early years were difficult. I was a young widow, but I always believed that God was with me. I prayed, "God, with You, I can make it."

I went back to school at Madonna University to get certified as a nurse in Michigan. I would find places to hide from my kids so that I could study for my board exam. I spent many long nights at Henry Ford Centennial Library while my mother watched the children. I graduated and passed my exam in spring of 1991.

The next challenge was to find a flexible job to make sure that my kids were taken care of. My mom was of great help, but she did not speak English. I had to be available for parent-teacher meetings, for programs which might be offered throughout the school day and for emergencies.

I had applied for several positions and had been offered various jobs but could not take them because of my need to be flexible. Providence led me to run into an old friend at a drug store. She had just started working for a local home healthcare agency. She offered to have me come shadow and apply for an open position. I have now worked as a homecare nurse in Metro Detroit for almost 30 years. We moved into a new house in December 1994 in west Dearborn. It was a blessing and still is.

Faith and education were the foundations of my parenting. Despite how busy I was working to provide for my family, I made it a priority to have family Bible study time. In the summer I insisted that my children read, and then I had them write book reports. We made time to walk the neighborhood and interact with the neighbors; I found that you can learn a lot from other people's stories.

I am fortunate to have three successful children. I had high expectations for them, and they really turned out well. Their high school principal once said to me, "How many times did you read to them? How frequently did you go to the library? We want more kids just like them!"

Priscila is the head of an Infection Prevention and Epidemiology department at a hospital. Jonathan is a computer science engineer. Ema is an optometrist and new young mother. They are involved in community service activities in the local and global community. Priscila has served as a public health worker in Africa and traveled with her brother on various service projects. Ema has volunteered in Latin America in eye ministry.

I have been blessed and am thankful. As I get ready for retirement, I am entering a new stage of life as a grandmother and hope to enjoy gardening.

I believe if you are blessed to be in America, it is up to you to work hard and bless others!

Udo Chiaramonti *still lives at his home in Dearborn Heights, Michigan. He enjoys visiting with his children and grandchildren, watching television (especially the Science channel) and doing crossword puzzles.*

The photo is of Udo as a young man in the late 1940s.

26

Udo Chiaramonti

I GREW UP NORTH OF FLORENCE, Italy. In my town it was difficult to find jobs and everybody wanted to come to the US. I liked my dad because he tried to get everyone a job. He came to the United States in 1925, leaving the rest of the family in his mother country. I did not see my dad again until 1932. In Italy he had built a 16-room house. He had two brothers in the Italian army. The Communists, Fascists, and Socialists were vying for power. Mussolini was the head of state.

I became a tailor in Italy, but few could afford custom-made suits, so I had to look around for other jobs. Among my first jobs was breaking stones for streets. I came to the US in 1947. My dad was working as a carpenter for the Briggs Corporation. I then took a job working for Pepsi Cola Corporation. I made 90 cents an hour stacking bottles. Among my side hustles was making piggy banks from plaster for five cents each.

Later, I worked for Hudson Motor Car Company, which then combined with Nash to become American Motors Corporation. I would work three or four hours a day on the assembly line for $1.50 per hour, hardly enough to get by on.

My days of making piggy banks got me a job working for Ford Motor Company. I became a clay model maker and spent 47 years working there. I was happy every minute of it. There has always been competition within the design area of Ford Motor. Of the products that I worked on was the Edsel. I quit my job at Ford to work at International Truck in Indianapolis because my pay jumped from $450 to $650 per month. I recognized my error and returned to my job at Ford Motor Company.

I bought a home in Dearborn Heights, just 12 blocks from my place of employment. My wife, Marta Angione, and I met on the boat going from Italy to the US. I remember my father-in-law's first words to me (and they were not friendly): "Who gave you permission to take my daughter out?" But Marta and I married and had six children. They are all honest and hardworking. Alex is a dermatologist, Luisa is a nurse, Gracie is a stay-at-home mom, Annette is a hairdresser, Carl is an accountant, and George has physical issues and cannot work.

I am proud of my family. I had a good marriage which lasted until my wife passed away. In other words, I had a good life!

Ed Demerly

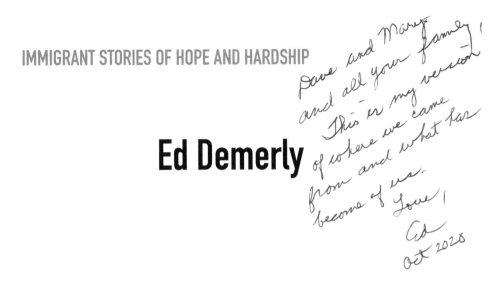

Dave and Mary and all your family! This is my version of where we came from and what has become of us.

Love,
Ed
Oct 2020

I GUESS IT ALL STARTED with Napoleon. During his European conquests, the German/French border area of Alsace and Lorraine was a major military route and battleground. Many young men were killed, but the population soon grew with families of 10 to 12 children. My direct ancestors had 16 children, though several died at a very young age. Within a couple generations, this area of Lorraine, France, lacked enough food and work to survive adequately.

Thus, on June 21, 1832, Jacob Demmerle, age 57, and his wife Marie, left Le Havre Harbor in northern France on a ship named *James* with nine of their children. My great-great-grandfather, Andrew, came with them at the age of 24. They intended to settle in Buffalo but eventually arrived in New Collins in western New York by way of the Erie Canal. Andrew later purchased 58 acres of land from the Holland Company for $246 in 1837, and with his father, became successful farmers. In the process of immigration, family members were given various spellings of their last name depending on the immigration agent who registered them; thus, we have in our extended family Demerly, Demerle, Demmerley, and Demmerle.

Andrew and his wife, Magdalena, had seven children. Strangely enough, several of these children were registered on official records with the last name spelled Demerle and the others as Demerly. There were four sons, two named Nicholas. As I understand it, the older Nicholas, my great grandfather, left New York for Benzonia, Michigan in his early 20s after a

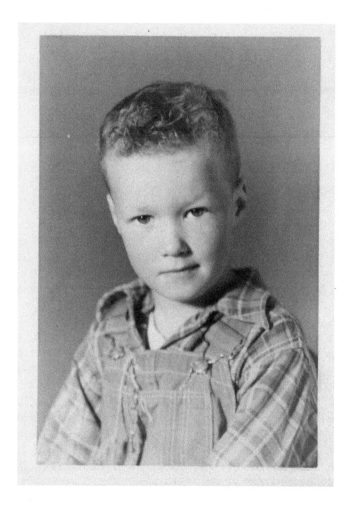

Ed Demerly *is a fourth generation French/German immigrant with Scottish ancestry on his mother's side. He has visited over thirty countries and lived and worked in Malaysia and Australia. He taught English for 46 years, primarily at Henry Ford College.*

The photo of Ed is from kindergarten while attending Perry Consolidated schools, Perry Michigan, in 1945.

family dispute about farm property inheritance. There apparently wasn't enough land to divide among four sons. For generations within the family, there was no discussion about the New York relatives, and none of the family ever returned to visit those relatives. My great-grandfather homesteaded land that had been timbered and developed a quite prosperous farm. He donated a small section of his farm for a local one-room schoolhouse and in gratitude, the county named the road on which he lived Demerly Road, which still crosses M-31 about a mile south of Benzonia today. His oldest son, Andrew, inherited the farm Nicholas had homesteaded.

Nicholas and his wife, Hannah, who was born in the Netherlands, had seven children, five who lived to adulthood. The oldest, another Andrew, was my grandfather. Andrew bought land adjoining the farm Nicholas homesteaded. This is where my dad and my older brother were born. Because he lived across the state and died when I was four years old, I don't have any memories of him. However, I do remember his wife Josephine, my Grandma Demerly, who died when I was nine. After Andrew's death, she lived with her daughter a couple miles from my childhood home. My mother says she was a wonderfully kind, affable, and generous woman, but the memories of my siblings and me would contest that. Our memories were of a mean old grandma who, if we didn't "pipe down" at nap time, threatened to spank us with the "pancake flopper," and other times she sent us to get "willar switches" to whip us. She had raised seven children and was in her sixties when she occasionally babysat us five children, all born within seven years. I'm sure she wasn't about to put up with any nonsense. My one fond memory was that in apple harvest season, she had all five of us sit on the floor in a circle around her as she sat peeling apples. She peeled an apple in one long spiral and fed us the peel one at a time as if we were little birds being fed worms.

My father, Shirley, the youngest of his parents' seven children, was 21 years younger than his oldest brother. I understand there were several miscarriages between live births. After eighth grade, my dad ended his formal education and left that same one-room school his grandfather had donated to the township. I'm told it was because he needed to find work during the Depression, but it may have been that he was tired of his mother's watching his every move in the classroom from her kitchen window. He worked at a dairy, harvested ice from Crystal Lake in winter, cut timber, picked fruit, and worked for other farmers. Eventually, he found work as a farmhand about 100 miles to the south near Owosso, where he met my mother at a barn dance where he was playing guitar in a country band. My mother, Dorothy, was a town girl with a high school education. Her father was a poor country lawyer and county prosecutor who was sometimes paid with chickens and vegetables during the Depression. Her mother was a one-room schoolteacher before she married. I don't remember either of them because they died when I was very young. They were of Wilson/Ford Scottish ancestors who immigrated before the American revolution; not, however, the Woodrow and Henry branches of the Scottish tree.

My parents returned to Benzonia for three years after their marriage and lived with my grandparents where my older brother was born. With luck in his work as an attorney, my Grandpa Wilson was able to find and put a down payment on a foreclosed 120-acre farm near Owosso—a gift for them in place of the college education my mother's three siblings were given. I was the first of their five children, born in Owosso in 1941, making me a fourth-generation immigrant. That farm is now managed by my brother, his son, and his grandson.

My father was a phenomenally successful, proud, creative farmer. He was fortunate to be farming in prosperous, post-war 1950s America, but I remember poverty in my first ten years, living in a two-room converted granary with a wood-burning kitchen stove, one running faucet, an outdoor toilet, an icebox, and a sometimes-leaky roof. My parents started farming with horses and a few chickens, pigs, and dairy cattle. Little by little, with increased bank loans that worried my mother, they were able to build a new home and sheds from lumber timbered from the farm and to buy improved machinery and more livestock. With three teenage sons to help with farmwork in these years, life improved for all of us. My sisters and mother contributed immeasurably as well, often doing the barn chores during harvesting while we were in the fields, not to mention laundry, sewing, cooking, trips to town for machinery parts, and bookkeeping. Farm life was a family lifestyle, not a job.

All five of us children completed high school. My older brother, David, served in the army then worked for years as a foreman in construction. I completed my master's degree in English after having served in the Army and the Peace Corps. I taught for 46 years, mostly at Henry Ford College. My younger brother, Dick, took over the farm and with the help of his youngest son and now, his grandson, has expanded the business considerably. My sister Judy worked as a secretary for a Congressman, and later, owned her own seamstress business, then worked in a dental office. My younger sister, Sally, also owns her own seamstress business, making wedding gowns, curtains, and suits. She also does some missionary work in Brazil and the Philippines.

As for my parents' great grandchildren, sixth-generation immigrants, there are an engineer, financial planners, business owners, a horticulturist, a farmer, teachers, an event planner, a homecare nurse, a psychologist, a geologist, a graphic designer, and a construction planner.

In 2006, I visited the small village of Etting, Lorraine, France, the first ancestor of emigres to the USA to return to the village from which they came 174 years earlier. In 2005, Gilles Demmerle, a distant relative and family genealogist I'd never heard of contacted me by email inquiring about my ancestry, of which I knew almost nothing beyond my parents. He however, knew much—going back about four centuries. When he heard that we planned to travel to Europe the following year, his research of my branch of the Demmerles began in earnest.

He and I first met in the High Tyrol Mountains of Austria and traveled to the mountain village of Strengen, where we had dinner with the Tamerl family who had lived at the same homesite for over 400 years. When some of that family of stonecutters moved around 1679 to Germany and France after the Thirty Years War during the reign of King Louis XIV, their name became Demmerle. Christian Tamerl from Zams, Austria, settled first in Achen, Germany, in1681 then moved to Etting, France, in 1708.

Our journey ended at a reunion, to my surprise, in the town hall of Etting with about 200 Demerly relatives, the town mayor, and French public television. I have returned to that village several times since then and have maintained friendships with a number of my new relatives who have also visited the US. On my last visit, while walking in the local cemetery with my wife, Martha, where a third of the plots seemed to be Demmerles, we met another Martha Demmerle visiting a relative's grave. It's a small world.

My family's immigration story isn't complete without including my adopted Korean daughter, Angela, who arrived at age five in 1975, just as American involvement in the Vietnam War was ending. Even before her arrival, I sensed some of the racial resentment she might face as she grew older. As my wife and I were announcing to my aunt and uncle our intention to adopt, my uncle seemed not to hear that we were adopting a Korean child. He went on to expound quite strongly how he couldn't understand parents who adopted foreign children instead of seeking a child who might look like themselves. Soon after her arrival, Angela was in the supermarket with me when a stranger, thinking that she was Vietnamese, told me, "You know, you are robbing her of her culture." Several years later while traveling to Florida during a school break, we stopped for a quick lunch at a family restaurant in Kentucky. We had agreed to order something that wouldn't take long so that we could get back on the road. In the restaurant, we were greeted and brought water and Cokes and placed our orders. After waiting interminably as others who came after us were being served, I asked the server about our order. She said she'd check but never returned. I went to the kitchen to inquire but got no response. I thought that if we got up to leave, someone would come running with a bill for the Cokes. We did leave without any notice from the staff. It was only later that I felt we surely weren't served because Angela was with us.

In her elementary school, Angela's classmates found her difference unique and easily befriended her, although she did hear taunts from a few bullies who stretched their eyelids into slanted positions and called her "Chinese eyes." She attended a much more racially diverse middle school and high school where her best friends were black students.

Angela completed her bachelor's degree in global finance and education and has worked in banking. She and her Irish American husband have three beautiful daughters, including twins, and their older sister who will soon start college at the University of Cincinnati.

My embrace of diversity seems not so much due to my family's immigration history but as a result of my exposure to racial equity in the military, my life as an "immigrant" serving in the Peace Corps in Malaysia for two years, as well as the influence of Dr. Martin Luther King during the Civil Rights Movement in the 1960s. I grew up in a farm community, isolated from racial diversity. As a child, I was totally unaware of the Polish, Czech, and German names of my classmates. I had never seen a black person until I was in high school, when on our way to visit an aunt and uncle, we passed through an area in Flint that had been destroyed by a tornado. Also while in high school, my family traveled to Florida to visit friends. I recall so well the signs of segregation. In college, I met and made friends with students of other races. My parents never identified people by race, and my mother especially enjoyed meeting my Asian and black friends when they visited the farm.

In my wife's extended family and mine, we have multiple European ethnicities, as well as Mexican, Iranian, Native American, African American, Korean, and Thai. I feel blessed with our family's diversity.

Imam Mohammad Ali Elahi *is the spiritual leader of the Islamic House of Wisdom in Dearborn Heights, Michigan, one of the largest religious institutions in the State of Michigan. He is a prolific writer and a media personality. He earned a bachelor's degree in sociology from the University of Michigan Dearborn and a master's degree in art from Wayne State University in Detroit. Over the years, Imam Elahi has received the endorsement from some of the highest religious authorities in the Muslim world and numerous awards and recognitions for his outreach and progressive religious and social services both locally and nationally.*

Imam Mohammad Ali Elahi

I TRAVELED TO THE UNITED STATES the very first time during the summer of 1990. At that time, I worked at the Tehran Times newspaper as a writer and clergyman, writing about religious events according to the Islamic calendar. Prior to working at the Tehran Times, I lived in London for about a year to take language classes to improve my English.

One day while working at the newspaper, we received a letter from the Assembly of World Religions. They requested a representative to attend an interfaith conference that involved people from well-known faith societies around the world. The conference was to be held in San Francisco. The letter was not addressed to a specific person, so any of the existing writers could apply. They were looking for a religious leader or a clergyman. There was another clergyman at the paper, assistant editor Mohammad Bakar Ansari, but he was not interested since there was no American embassy in Tehran, and it was difficult to obtain a visa. The relationship between the two countries was tense after the Islamic revolution in Iran. I decided to apply. I called the conference center in New York and spoke with Dr. Thomas Walsh. I informed him of my interest and asked for the invitation to be addressed in my name.

I took the invitation to the American Embassy at the UAE in Abu Dhabi in the United Arab Emirates. There was a long line, but I finally obtained the application and waited for the visa interview. The person who interviewed me asked what the conference was about, and I simply said, "It's about God!" I answered his questions very briefly, but after a long interview and questions about what I did in Tehran, the agent put a red stamp on my passport. My visa was denied. I was upset. I called the ambassador's office directly and was connected to his secretary. I explained the situation. She advised me to apply again the following day. I went to the consulate the next day and applied again. I interviewed once more, but this time he said he would send the application to Washington, D.C. to see what they had to say. He informed me that if they confirmed, I would get the visa. He gave me his phone number and told me to keep calling him because it might take up to a month.

A few days after my return to Tehran, I called every other day until they finally informed me that the visa was granted. They asked me to return to the embassy to have my passport stamped. I informed Dr. Walsh that I had gotten my visa and needed a plane ticket since it was provided by the conference. They sent the ticket to Lufthansa in Istanbul. They were also willing to reimburse me for my flight from Tehran to Istanbul.

Excited, I flew to Istanbul. My flight to San Francisco was out of Frankfort, but I was informed that I needed a transit visa. I took a taxi and went to the German consulate to obtain my transit visa to Germany. The flight to Frankfurt was the following day at 9 a.m., but I had to be at the airport by 7:00 a.m.

I reached the consulate at 4 p.m. I stood in a long line, but the consulate closed before my turn. This was my worst nightmare because the next flight to San Francisco was three days later, and I would miss four days of the five-day conference. I was frustrated and upset. The visa section closed around 5 p.m. I didn't know what to do. I stood at the gate and informed the guard that I was desperate.

Security informed me that was closed and to return the next day. I insisted that it was an emergency. Facing my insistence, they talked to the consul assistant, the only one who to my luck was still in her office. As she was coming down the hall, I could hear the echo of her shoes in the empty building. She told me to follow her to her office. She listened carefully. She was an angel.

She helped me fill out he application because it was in German, and I knew no German. However, she didn't have the transit visa stamp, so she granted me an actual German visitor's visa. I owed her 20 dollars. I mailed the money to her once I was back in Tehran.

America was my first international outreach. San Francisco had perfect weather, and as I was waiting for my transport to the hotel, I assumed America's weather was the same everywhere. The conference offered almost a week of lectures. I met and spoke to people from many places. In addition to the conference host, the late Rev. Moon, I met Sheikh Kaftaroo, then the grand mufti of Syria. We had a promising conversation. He said that if Sunni means to follow the Sunnah of the prophet, we are all Sunni, and if Shia means to love Ahlulbayt, the Prophet's family, then we are all Shia. The conference was at the Hyatt Regency Hotel, a new and magnificent building. I learned much and gained a lot of experience. I spoke at some workshops throughout the week.

When the conference was over, I decided to visit Muslim communities in the US. I learned that some airlines had a policy that if you were not a resident and were traveling for pleasure, you could buy a $400 ticket for one month of unlimited flights on Delta. During that month I traveled to Los Angeles, Washington DC, Texas, New York City, and stopped in Detroit, not knowing much about it. I had heard that there were some Iranian Muslim students in the Detroit area. They picked me up from the airport, took me to their home and arranged meetings with Islamic centers, including the Islamic Center of America on Joy Road. The Islamic Center was interested in inviting me to be the Imam of the mosque because Imam Cherri was old and suffering from Alzheimer's. They were excited that I knew English. We exchanged phone numbers for future correspondence once I returned to Iran.

Six or seven months later, the late Hajj Khalil Alawan wrote a letter inviting me to an interfaith conference that he was holding at the Islamic Center. He wanted me to present on leadership in Islam. I applied for a visa, but this time it was approved because I had developed some travel history. I went to America, visited for a few days, and returned to Iran.

Our correspondence continued till 1992, the year I moved to Michigan. I became the Imam and spiritual director of the Islamic Center of America.

My journey to the US started with interfaith studies. It was one of my main interests. I decided to make interfaith a permanent part of my mission.

At the end of a three-year contract with the Islamic Center of America, I left and established the Islamic House of Wisdom (IHW) the same year in 1995. For the first two years, we held our services at a hall in Dearborn that is known today as the Byblos Banquet Hall. In 1997, we purchased the Detroit World Outreach Church in Dearborn Heights to where we transitioned the IHW site shortly thereafter. During the same year, I held a national interfaith conference where leaders from Washington, D.C., including Rabbi David Saperstein and the national leader of the Christian faith. It was a humbling experience.

A few months later, with the help of Imam Abdallah el-Amin, an African American imam and the founder of the Muslim Center in Detroit, we held the first ever Shia-Sunni unity conference at IHW.

Today, one of the strongest dimensions of IHW is interfaith dialogue. We do everything that a mosque does: prayer, family services, Arabic and Farsi schools, girl scouts, boy scouts, classes for youth and ladies, outreach, helping the poor, distribution of food, outreach to media and honoring Islamic occasions, but interfaith has been an area of focus from its conception.

Celebrating similarities, appreciating differences, working together toward a world of peace, justice, empathy and understanding is a rewarding experience. We see interfaith dialogue as an instrument of education, especially when our faith is totally misunderstood and the disease of Islamophobia and hatred is hurting not only Muslims, but also the image and interests of our country.

We have a rich history of interfaith dialogue. For example, we talk about Prophet Mohammed's family, traditions, the Charter of Medina, and the interfaith letters of the prophet to the leaders of the world during his time. From my initial interfaith mission in 1990 to my recent Interfaith Summit of 2020 in Seoul, South Korea, I knew that interfaith dialogue is worthwhile!

On February 4, 2020, over 6000 religious and political leaders and peace activists from around the globe, including myself, participated in an interfaith summit in Seoul, South Korea. H.E. Ban Ki-moon, former UN Secretary-General and Bishop Munib Younan of the Lutheran Church from the Holy Land were among the Summit Award Recipients of this amazing global gathering, organized and hosted by "Universal Peace Federation."

This is one of my presentations at the Seoul conference:

"Let's start with a silent prayer for the victims of the coronavirus everywhere in the world and with an expression of solidarity for the various suffering cities from China to the USA and other suffering areas in the world.

Please remember that Mr. Ross, the US Commerce Secretary, did not speak for all Americans when he said the coronavirus creates more jobs in America; he was adding insult to injury.

It's an honor to be part of this 2020 summit of world religions in Seoul.

My first journey to America, from Tehran to Istanbul to Frankfurt to San Francisco, marked my first participation in AWR (Assembly of World Religions). Over 500 distinguished world leaders and interfaith activists met from August 15–21 1990 at the Hyatt Regency Hotel. Today, when I saw Dr. Tom Walsh speaking, I remembered him from the San Francisco conference 30 years earlier. Later, I met with Dr. Rev. Jenkins, Bishop Stalin, and other shining stars in this spiritual galaxy of grace and friendship.

Now thirty years later, over 6000 guests in Seoul are meeting to share their wisdom and discuss their vision of global peace in a world filled with various threats such as nuclear weapons, climate crisis, health concerns, and cyber-attacks.

I listened to Rev. Moon, the founder of Universal Peace Federation (UPF), in that world conference 30 years ago, spoke about the philosophy of creation and he answered the question: why did God create us? His answer was that it was not for the purpose of money or power, but love; divine love, family love and love of neighbors.

At one time during that summit I was walking with the late Dr. Ahmad Kuftaro, then the mufti of Syria, and I told him that Imam Jafar al-Sadeq said, "Is religion anything but love?" What is faith without love, sacrifice, compassion, hope, humbleness, prayer and charity?

That trip to San Francisco was a miracle. Years later, I realized I was on a mission from God without knowing it. At that time, I was wondering if they had some sort of agenda by inviting me. Did they want to convert me? Impose a political agenda? Debating, arguing, judging, or blaming my spiritual belief system? No, not at all! Their purpose was to get together, talk to each other, and to see together how we could make a better world, a world of peace.

What a great way to honor one of the best names of Allah— "Peace"—and also recognize the international ISLAMIC salutation of "salaam."

How can we bring peace to a world suffering from war, violence, crime, corruption, confusion, pain, poverty, extremism, terrorism, intolerance, misunderstanding, misconception, deception, dishonesty? The first step is dialogue; people of wisdom and dignity from all over the world meeting to share ideas for world peace.

Dialogue is one of the main messages of the Quran.

1. O people of faith join us for a journey of interfaith to recognize the central truth in this universe.
2. Through this dialogue we start knowing one another.
3. Do this conversation with maximum beauty, courtesy, respect and wisdom.
4. The goal is to cooperate for what is good for humanity.
5. It's about competition for compassion, and acts of kindness.
6. It's about making reconciliation,

forgiveness, friendship and being one family of humanity.

7. It's about protection of places of prayer, building bridges of brotherhood, understanding and good relationships for the sake of peaceful coexistence.

8. The obstacles of peace that must be rejected are oppression, discrimination, racism, greed, ignorance, ego and arrogance. These things are poisonous for peace. At the same time, we must adopt a language of love, respect, tolerance, patience, modesty and humility.

9. Last but not least, in order to bring a peaceful coexistence, we must stand for justice; justice in our expressions, actions, judgments, even if justice hurts ourselves and helps our enemies.

10. If there had been such a dialogue, human history would not have suffered from 200 years of bloody and brutal Crusades in the Holy Land, World War I, World War II, the Vietnam War, Iraq War, Afghanistan War, Yemen War, Syrian War and over 70 years of the Israeli-Palestinian conflict.

I hope our leaders learn from those deadly and destructive wars and stop their warmongering and choose the blessing of being ambassadors of peace and justice. We cannot establish true peace if we fail to establish justice.

I conclude by remembering the words of the late Martin Luther King, Jr..`

"Injustice anywhere is a threat to justice everywhere" and, "We must learn to live together as brothers, or we are going to perish together as fools."

૭ ❀ ৩

I flew back home—the United States— from South Korea and suffered from the interrogation and insults of immigration officials at Detroit Metro Airport. I was shocked since I was a law-abiding citizen and had lived in Michigan for over 30 years. The next day I led Friday prayer at the mosque and flew to Washington D.C. to participate in a Shia Sunni scholar's forum. I thought traveling domestically, I wouldn't face the same harassment as an international trip, yet I faced the same painful profiling!

Today, as an American citizen and a citizen of the world and father of seven beautiful children, some married and some still young, we live a beautiful family life.

Overall, I am proud of my country of origin, the Islamic Republic of Iran, and the country of my destination, the United State of America. The beautiful country that has given me the opportunity to live, to serve and to enjoy my freedom of expression and religious liberty. America is not totally free from Islamophobia, racism and other shortcomings, but it's blessed with so many people of integrity and consciousness. With continuity of our dialogue, interaction, engagement and sense of cooperation and solidarity, we will make America, a better place for generations to come.

God willing — Enshaallah.

Ana Marie (Cedillos) Gierhart

IMMIGRATION IS A HOT TOPIC these days. It is unusual to turn on the news without hearing something about it. Many times, immigration is written and spoken about in a negative light using assumptions or stereotypes that do not allow for truth to shine through. When I watch the news, it seems that most stories have ulterior motives. Whether the news venue is trying to boost ratings with controversial stories or trying to promote a political platform, much of what is featured doesn't seem authentic to me.

I hope that my story will not seem tainted by controversy or a political aim. I want to share some truths and shed some light about immigration issues in the United States. I want the American people to know that there are immigrants who are deserving of their status. There are immigrants here who are quite thankful and appreciative of the chance they have been given to pursue their version of the American Dream.

My story starts in the country of El Salvador, Central America, in a little village called La Pintada. I lived on land mostly owned by my maternal grandfather. My dream of going to America began when I was a young girl and heard the stories of others who traveled to America to visit relatives. I was desperate to get away from an abusive mother and the neglect, abandonment, and poverty that surrounded me. I wanted to change my world and the world of my five siblings. By the time I was a

This is Ana at 17 *in her high school photo just prior to her journey to America. Later in her life the rest of her siblings joined her in the United States. She enjoyed a flourishing nursing career and is now retired in Ft. Worth with her husband, Mickey, an anesthesiologist. Below is Ana today.*

teenager, the Salvadoran Civil War of the late 1970s and the early '80s left me disillusioned. I personally witnessed the atrocities of war, and these atrocities were applied even to aspiring young girls whose only crime was the aspiration for a university education but who instead became victims of rape and even mutilation and murder. I did not think it possible to achieve my dreams of becoming a doctor in my own country. I saw bodies at the side of the road as I walked to catch a school bus to my high school. I could not believe my eyes and my young heart bled and cried to witness these tragedies. I also lost family members. Two of my female cousins were killed while they studied at the university.

But the silver lining of these monumental tragedies in my country was the strengthening of my resolve to leave. The United States of America was my symbol of hope and my destination. I almost went to Canada instead because that great country was giving asylum to Salvadorans, but there was an opportunity awaiting me to come to the beautiful America I have come to adore!

I was visiting my aunt and she introduced me to a 14-year-old girl who had been kicked out of a relative's home along with her little brother. Her parents were already in the US. I invited this girl to come to my home and she agreed. A few months later my young friend's father came to pick up her and her brother, and she campaigned for her dad to bring me to America also. Witnessing some of my abuse at home had stimulated this request. The father told me that if I could find $300.00, a substantial amount of money in my country, he would be willing to try. I finally found the money!

The day to leave arrived in 1984 when I was eighteen. We left bright and early one morning . The trip was long; first, we arrived in Guatemala City and spent the night. The next day, we boarded a plane to Monterrey, Mexico. The passport my friend's father acquired for me carried me closer to America, but the last part of the trip would be more dangerous. We stayed in Monterrey a while longer with a friend of my friend's father's family named Doña Mariquita, who fed us the most outstanding breakfasts. We stayed there until we could find a smuggler to take us into the United States.

My friend and her family left first, so I had to continue alone, though I had the family's contact information. I crossed the Rio Grande with the help of the smuggler. Finding a phone, I tried calling the mother of the family but she did not want to help, so I approached a taxi driver who said he would take me to Houston, where a friend lived, for another $300.00, which I did not have. Fortunately, my friend knocked on doors of neighbors when we arrived past midnight and was able to come up with enough money to satisfy the driver.

My story did not end there. Before I left, my dear friends and classmates tried to persuade me not to leave. They argued that if I left my country and my studies, my dreams of becoming a doctor would be very slim. They also warned me that if I left, I was more likely to become a housekeeper, a nanny, or a dishwasher. I did not end in a low-paying job though I certainly held many in my quest for my dream.

But a fortune cookie changed my life. You may be wondering how I could make such a bold statement. I worked at a Chinese restaurant as a dishwasher and as I collected the dishes, there was a fortune cookie on each plate! Some were cracked, some were intact, but what caught my attention was not the cookie itself but the message they carried within. This would change my life! I collected the fortune cookie messages from every table, and every dish, placing them inside a small trash bag. And at the end of my work shift, I went home carrying my trash bag full of the little messages I called treasures. At home I had a legal pad in which I would trace a vertical line. In the first space, I penned word by word the messages from the fortune cookies and then translated them on the next space with the help of a Spanish – English dictionary that I still own to this day. I saw this as an opportunity to learn

English. I knew that if I lived in America, I would to have to know English well in order to succeed. This was truly the beginning of a life-changing opportunity for me. This small step impacted my life and gave me the desire to keep striving.

I even applied to a vocational training program. Advertised on TV, it solicited bilingual students. Oh, how bilingual I was. Not really! I was denied of course, but I did not give up. I am not ashamed to tell you that I begged the coordinator to let me into the program even if on a trial basis. She agreed, not without first warning me that if I was not performing to the levels required by the program, that I was going to be immediately cut off from both the grant and the program. I was very happy she allowed me the opportunity to try. I am delighted to report that I excelled in every class I took, and my teachers appreciated my every effort and encouraged me along the way. I even wrote an essay portraying myself as my own hero. I am not trying to be pretentious here; I had to be my own hero on many occasions.

I was totally in the program, but now there was another challenge. For me to get into college, I had to earn my GED. I lacked half a year for my high school diploma. My coordinator informed me that I could go to the library to get the Spanish version of the books needed to study for my GED. So, I decided to challenge myself and read the GED books in English. It was truly difficult, but I diligently studied day and night in order to learn all that I needed to be prepared for my test. I remember the day before the date for me to take the test; I was pretty nervous and I approached the supervisor of my coordinator, the director of the program whom I grew to love and appreciate for his sweet disposition and his encouragement. I told him how nervous I felt to which he replied "Ana Marie, when you are ready to take the test, repeat to yourself, this test is mine." May he ever be blessed for how those words encouraged me to test with confidence. To my huge surprise I passed the English version of my GED. I was leaping with joy! I was one step closer to entering college. My coordinator was also happy that I passed but now she had yet another challenge waiting for me. Foreign students applying for college in America must pass a pre-entrance test called the TOEFL (test of English as a foreign language) and, of course, it is given in English. There are four sections that take a total of about 4 1/2 hours to complete. During the test, the student is asked to perform tasks combining all four communication skills—reading, listening, speaking, and writing—in English. I passed the TOEFL and was again ecstatic!

I graduated with a surgical nursing degree from Houston Community College. This gave me the opportunity to work hand in hand with incredible people in the surgical units of the medical center hospitals in the city of Houston, Texas. At the very beginning of my career, the Texas Children's Hospital captured my heart. I had fallen in love with pediatric surgery when doing part of my clinical rotations there as a student and I worked there for six years. I became highly trained in every surgical specialty, but I had my favorites: ophthalmology and otolaryngology became specialties I loved!

I am grateful to have been a part of many great teams that not only enriched my life but also encouraged me to be the best that I could be. As a young girl, I always wanted to be a medical doctor. That dream seemed to be shattered when I left my country. But I was given many opportunities in the field of medicine, adding to the lives of thousands of people I met and worked with. I would have never in my life imagined working with incredible world-renown doctors and wonderful medical personnel in a foreign land I now call my home.

In sharing my fortune cookie story, I want to say that there are times in life when opportunities come knocking on our door or appear right in front of our eyes. Overlooking them may be the difference between a good life and an amazing life.

I want the American people to know that there are immigrants who are deserving of the American

Dream. There are immigrants here very thankful and appreciative of the chance they are given to live their real-life American Dream. We come here from our native countries with shattered dreams to look for bigger dreams in this great nation.

I would also remind people that as an immigrant, I made sure that I paid my income taxes on time and I know that other immigrants willingly paid taxes and followed all the laws of this great country, the United States of America. We want to make this our home and feel safe here. We come here to escape many issues we don't talk about because we are too busy setting down new roots here!

I am but one of those immigrants who has had a long journey to reach this point. I realize that I must share my story with you all and also tell you of how grateful and thankful I am to be here in the United States. I have officially been a citizen of our country since 2000.

Thank you!

This photo is of Steve Gierhart's grandparents, *Ruby and Lew, during the Depression in 1930 Oklahoma. His father, Lew Dale, is the baby and the young boy is his Uncle Gene who is still alive in Ft. Worth, Texas. Steve lives near Huntsville, Alabama on a horse farm with his wife, Bonny, after a long career as a civilian business director for the US Army.*

Steve Gierhart

THE GIERHART FAMILY is proud of their German heritage, even as we, like most Americans, realize that we are a mix of other cultures and nations as well. In our family's past are also English and French names. Our last name may also have changed over the centuries. Included may have been "Gerhart" or "Gearhart." We owe the knowledge and appreciation of our past to our father, Lew Dale Gierhart, a man born in the Great Depression but with a rich family history.

The greater Gierhart family also acknowledges the persistence and drive of Mark Gierhart of Lima, Ohio, who has amassed a large amount of genealogical history over the decades and incorporated it all into a national data base using Brothers Keeper Software. Mark linked our branch of the Gierhart family to his. Through his efforts we know that our family started with the arrival of Eitel (Also spelled Eytel and even Idel) Elias Gierhart (Gerhart). Eitel arrived in Philadelphia on September 21, 1751 at the age of 30. He was born in Rotterdam, Zuid-Holland, Netherlands on August 10, 1721 and after immigrating settled in Washington County, Maryland where he died in 1805. Eitel's father, Johann Heinrich Gierhart, was born on February 25, 1683 in Wolferborn, Hessen, Germany.

From this beginning our family moved westward as our country grew, like most Americans. Brothers Daniel and Henry, sons of Eitel, moved to Ohio sometime between 1805-1809. We know that our immediate branch takes off from Henry H. Gierhart who was born in Fairfield County, Ohio on December 29, 1809 and was a son of Daniel.

Our family has no giant of history, but we are proud of our accomplishments. Chaney R. Gierhart, a grandson of Henry H., was a soldier in the Civil War who was granted the honor of accompanying the body of Abraham Lincoln on its multiple train stops for citizens along the way to his final resting place in Springfield, Illinois. Articles from old Oklahoma newspapers reflect this in his obituary.

From Henry H. our branch moved further west to Indiana, then, as the 19th turned to the 20th century, resettled to the promised lands of Indian Territory, now Oklahoma. It was in the small town of Asher, Oklahoma that my dad, Lew Dale, was born on August 30, 1929. My grandfather, Lew Andrew, my dad's father, was one of the courageous Oklahomans known as "Okies" who had to work in California during the Depression, sending money home to their impoverished families, in our case to our grandmother Ruby Helen, who had two young boys to take care of. Life was hard but not insurmountable. They owe that courage to immigrant descendants.

A thread common to recent immigrants, especially those who entered the country illegally, is fear of deportation, even as most Americans forget their families arrived as immigrants with the same yearnings of immigrants of today. At what point do many Americans forget that fact, take it for granted, and somehow elevate ourselves to be better than those arriving today? Maybe part of it is simple human nature, the fear of change. Caucasian Americans with roots in Europe identify with a western culture which contrasts with the diversity of the world made in a melting pot of technology and transportation, a world where it is impossible for us not to mix cultures.

Maybe we should simply stop and realize that regardless of race or culture, at heart humans can be good, generous and dependable, leaning on each other where needed. Signs of acceptance surround us but to some are signals that things are awry when, instead, they are simply evolving. Let's hope we can continue this evolution with courage, with empathy, and understanding. After all, our values of family, hard work, and responsibility should power that evolution, not fear of the veneer of color, religion, and culture. Let us never forget that we are all immigrants. Only Native Americans can claim a lack of an immigrant past, and maybe some Native Americans are glad of it since hate, prejudice, and betrayal by the conquering forces in the Americas drove their isolation and destruction. We should be very afraid of hate and prejudice, cognizant of its hidden presence in us all, not making them cornerstones of a divisive political atmosphere with goals driven by fear of change.

Geraldine Grunow *has been married to Ken Grunow for forty-seven years. The photo of them is from their wedding. They have three children and five grandchildren. After teaching at Henry Ford Community College for twenty-seven years, Geraldine is retired and now lives in Dearborn. She is one of the coordinators of the Detroit Chapter of Amnesty International. She enjoys reading and writing (of course!), as well as baking and cooking.*

Geraldine Grunow

I GREW UP IN EDINBURGH, SCOTLAND, fortunate to live in an era of free public education, including university level. As I still do, I loved listening to the radio; one of my favorite programs was Alistair Cooke's Letter from America, which was first aired in 1946, a year before I was born. This series of weekly essays on American life engendered an interest in and love for the United States, especially for what I perceived then to be a commitment to diversity, a tolerance for unpopular views, and a generous optimism about the future. President Kennedy's challenge to "Ask not what your country can do for you, but what you can do for your country," resonated with my friends and me as an inspiring complement to volunteer work we were doing in Edinburgh. After graduation, many of my friends joined organizations that sent volunteers overseas. I was sent to a Catholic junior seminary/high school in northern Ghana. It was there that I met my future husband, Ken, who had come from Dearborn Heights, at the invitation of the rector of the seminary.

After our two-year volunteer commitment was over, we decided to settle in the United States somewhat arbitrarily, but mostly because we hoped that it would be easier for Ken to find work here. The process of obtaining a green card (Permanent Resident Card) was painstaking but not impossible. After about a year in our cozy Hamtramck apartment and the birth of our first child, we applied to VISTA, a US-based program similar to Peace Corps. We had to supply eight references with our application, and we were disappointed not to hear from the program for a long time. Then we learned that our applications had been lost; we had to ask our colleagues, professors, and supervisors to write references again (no electronic files in those days) and we resubmitted our applications.

Geraldine *before her retirement as an English instructor at Henry Ford Community College.*

While we waited with increasing impatience, we wrote to the school in Ghana, offering to come back, even though this time it would be with a baby. With a sense of serious purpose, we went to the end of the street and mailed this letter. When we returned home, we found an official letter from VISTA in our mailbox asking us to come to Chicago for training! We couldn't think of a way to extract the letter from the USPS mailbox, so we decided to let fate run its course. In fact, the Ghanaian staff at the school welcomed our return, despite the difficulties Ghana was enduring because of drought and a failing economy. After two challenging but rewarding years in the same school, we said goodbye to Northern Ghana and started our journey back to the United States, stopping in Scotland to see my family. This stop was very pleasant for all of us, but we learned too late that we had been given bad advice by the American Embassy in Ghana. I should not have stayed out of the country for more than two years, so I had to reapply for a green card, a very lengthy but finally successful process.

After our return, I lived happily as a permanent resident of the United States, renewing my Alien Registration whenever needed and dutifully driving to the downtown Federal Building to seek official permission to travel outside the United States whenever I went back to Scotland to visit my family. I was the at-home parent while our three children grew up. I also worked as a volunteer in several capacities: a teacher for a Summer Bible School at the parish we attended; a server at a soup kitchen; a teacher for Literacy Volunteers of America. However, since about 1979, my husband and I have committed most of our energy and time to Amnesty International, a grassroots movement that defends human rights everywhere. I've felt privileged to be able to do this important work here without the many restrictions on free speech that exist in other countries.

I did, however, become increasingly disenchanted with some of the policies of this country, especially as I learned about its lethal interference in countries such as Chile, Guatemala, and the Philippines. Since I wasn't a citizen, I couldn't help effect political change in this country, so I began my application for citizenship. I prepared the forms carefully but found it impossible to pledge to defend the United States with arms. Such a requirement was a contradiction to pacifism, a way of life I admired in great Americans such as Martin Luther King and Dorothy Day. I was surprised and disappointed when my application was rejected for that reason—by an officer who was certain that "Martin Luther King wasn't a pacifist." I hired a lawyer to help with my appeal of this decision, and after a short hearing by a supervising officer, I was granted US citizenship. I realize, of course, that my experience of delay bears no comparison to the terrible, needless suffering of many refugees fleeing violence today.

I am profoundly grateful for the fulfilling life I've led here in the United States; I especially loved my twenty-seven years as an English instructor at Henry Ford Community College, one of the best-kept secret paths to success in higher education. I've kept my British passport, and I enjoy visiting my family and friends in Scotland as a citizen. In addition, my husband and I keep in touch with students and colleagues from Ghana. Finally, especially through my work with Amnesty International, I've appreciated being a citizen of the United States while remembering that we are all citizens of the world.

Kadie Bangura Hadid
(Anonymous)

I WAS BORN IN MAKENI, a small town in the West African country of Sierra Leone and first inhabited by indigenous African peoples at least 2,500 years ago. The country was colonized by freed slaves in 1787 until Britain made it a crown colony in 1808. My father, who is of Lebanese descent, left Lebanon in the mid-1950s to join in the diamond rush taking place in Sierra Leone. He married my mother—whose mother was African, and father was Lebanese. My mother was considered an African national because of her African blood. She had more political power than my father since he was 100 percent Lebanese. Dual nationalities were not allowed for those who did not have African blood.

As a child and teenager, I identified heavily with the Lebanese community even though I had African relatives on my maternal grandmother's side. Our African lineage was from the Malinke (also known as Mandinka or Mandingo) tribe. The tribe was established under the Mali Empire which rose to power in the thirteenth century and found its way to Sierra Leone in the late 1870s through settlers from neighboring Guinea. I never knew my Mandingo grandmother, as she died before I was old enough to spend time with her. I learned to empathize with the black race mostly because I grew up knowing I had black heritage, and that there seemed to be some sort of unjustified perception among some white Lebanese that they were superior to the black Africans. In hindsight, I realize now that this was part of worldwide bigotry at the time, and that some good people had been ignorantly raised with the wrong impressions. In any case, I feel my mixed heritage was a blessing that opened my young mind and protected it from bigotry and racism.

My mother and aunts had stories of the various challenges they faced as biracial children, but because they had a brother who became a well-known businessman with political clout, they were able to face those challenges more easily than others. As children of a widely respected Lebanese man who had married their African mother from a prominent tribal family, they realized that other biracial children with less respectable parentage did not fare as well in terms of Lebanese societal acceptance and inclusion.

My father was old school but fair-minded. He fully respected and supported my mother's position as a working mother. He ran a general goods store in town, while my mother did most of the traveling and cross border business dealings. Her father and brother were her "go to." They schooled her in the skill of purchasing and deal making, and she too became business savvy and successful in her own right. She gave birth to eight children.

As one of those eight children growing up, our parents taught us that no one person was better than the other because of skin color and/or level of wealth. Rather, our deeds would define our level of standing. We were encouraged to work hard to achieve material success, but also to do good and treat all others with respect, regardless of background.

During my early years, my four older siblings went to school in Lebanon since the schools in Sierra Leone advocated for vocational training over academia. In addition, my father wanted his children to learn how to speak, read, and write Arabic. Before I was old enough to join my siblings at the Makassed boarding school in Lebanon, the civil war broke out in 1975, and made it impossible. My parents sought my siblings and brought them home. Shortly thereafter, we moved to Freetown, the country's capital. Freetown had a more cosmopolitan feel, with a much larger and more affluent Lebanese expatriate community than Makeni. In Makeni, I had attended St. Joseph's Elementary school with mostly black students, but when in Freetown, I attended the Lebanese International Middle and High School with mostly Lebanese students.

Once out of high school where I graduated with honors, my parents sent me to London to live with my brother and his wife who had been living there for a few years. I obtained a Bachelor's in Computer Science from the University of London, all the while fully appreciating life in Great Britain, a developed western country, after a lifetime of living in Sierra Leone, a third world country. Nonetheless, as I got older, and life became harder, I fully appreciated the happy childhood, close-knit Lebanese community, and the simpler life we had had in Sierra Leone.

One of the many things I was receptive of while living in London was of certain indigenous tribal practices that I had heard about in vague whispers during my childhood. This included the abhorrent practice of female genital mutilation. This was a term I did not even learn until I was living in the West. I later understood what was occurring in some secret societal rites of passage that take place in African countries and other parts of the world. One such society had been known as the Bondo society. Female members from our domestic help, whom I grew up with, would disappear for lengthy periods of time and when I questioned where they had gone, I was vaguely told, they had gone to join the Bondo. Some of them came back, while others never did. I used to see dancing and festivities in the streets whenever these secret society rituals were over, but never realized the atrocities that had been committed on these female tribal members when they came of age. My parents never elaborated on the Bondo, simply saying that it was a society restricted to tribal members, and that its rituals were not based on religion (Islam and Christianity are the two main religions in Sierra Leone), but rather on ancient tribal traditions.

When I graduated from the university in London, I returned to Sierra Leone to be with my family and help my parents run their business. However, I married almost a year later to a Lebanese man from Sierra Leone, whose immediate family had moved to the United States.

He left ahead of me to start the immigration paperwork, while I waited amidst rumblings of the start of a civil war due to rebel incursions from neighboring Liberia. Within a year, I left Sierra Leone and entered the United States on a visitor's visa. While in the United States, civil war broke out in Sierra Leone, and I was able to gain temporary protected status (TPS) which came with work authorization. Several years after Immigration and Naturalization Services had misplaced my husband's citizenship application file, he was forced to resubmit the paperwork, adding further delays to the process. Throughout several years, I worked with my husband and his father in the wholesale business, while raising the three children we had been blessed with. I had a strong English background and when I first came to the US, I was surprised by the number of American born citizens who made grammatical and spelling mistakes. But what I loved most about America was how the public-school system embraced diversity and equality, and how kind and unpretentious in general most Americans were, at least in the Midwest. I admired how my children, along with the other students, were taught to treat everyone with kindness and respect. Of course, some of that changed after 911, and now many Arab Muslims live in fear of being stereotyped and treated with bias. However, I still saw many acts of kindness and respect from the community that helped alleviate the ugly effect of racism in its many forms.

After years of living on TPS status, and a twice divorced relationship that unsuccessfully tried to make it through irreconcilable differences, the person who had brought me to this country ironically lost his case for citizenship and returned to his original homeland. By association, Homeland Security began legal proceedings to remove me and the children from the country. My children were doing well in school, and I could not fathom the idea of leaving America, a country I had learned to embrace. All three of my children were US citizens, and with the help of an immigration lawyer and the testimonials of some caring and kind friends and family members, I was able to win my battle with Homeland Security. The immigration court granted me permanent resident status that eventually led to full citizenship. America allowed me to feel more of who I am, with respect to my personal values and faith. Amongst all the countries I had lived in, America is where I feel most at home. When my children's father left the country, we were dependent on him, and I sometimes wondered if I should have taken them to join him abroad. However, I knew subconsciously that they had a higher chance of securing a better future in America. They would have lost that advantage had I moved them back to an economically crippled third world country struggling to emerge from the ashes of a brutal civil war. I had always been an independent person and I knew that where there was a will, there was a way. While my children were blessed with some loving family members, and their father did his best to minimize the hardship his departure had caused, I knew that my choice to remain in America would change my life and my responsibilities as a single parent. With a degree in computer science but no experience, I pursued a career in Public Accounting. I worked days at a local accounting firm and studied nights to obtain a master's in accounting and gain CPA qualifications. I began my professional career in mid-life working at a renowned public accounting firm as an auditor. My children are successfully working on various university and career paths. After the life-changing experience of becoming a single parent household and having to almost leave this country for an uncertain future, my children and I fully grasp the value of hard work and determination.

We totally appreciate the blessings we have been given. I have done my best to teach the children to be productive citizens and to give back whenever they can. After all, this is the country that embraced me and gave me the opportunity to live an internally satisfying life.

Ernie Hassan *began his career at 11 when his parents opened Ernie's Market 65 years ago. He graduated from the University of Detroit with a bachelor's in science majoring in business which has aided him in becoming a successful businessman so loved by the community that he has been honored as the Good Will Ambassador of Oak Park. Everyday Ernie tries to change the world by making his customers' sandwiches with "Love" and sending them off with, "Who loves you Baby? Ernie does."*

The photo above is of his father, Ernie Senior (left), and Ernie (right) during a busy day outside the store during the 1980s. Ernie Senior worked every day until the day he died at 79 in 1991.

Ernie Hassan

A NAME SOMETIMES JUST "FITS" a person or even two in this case. According to the Merriam-Webster Dictionary, Earnest means sincerity or often zealousness of purpose.

Ernie Hassan I and Ernie Hassan II truly are earnest men, loved and revered by all.

On January 5, 1912, my father Mustafa Hassan was born in Quebec, Canada to Fatima and Hassan. Mustafa has always been known as "Ernest" or "Ernie" to his friends and family. He was the oldest boy and was taught from the time he was young to take charge and take care of his five sisters and his younger brother and later, his own family.

My grandfather's father had been a fur trader who became handicapped when the winter ice broke and he fell into the freezing lake water. Due to his injury, the family moved to Windsor and opened a corner market that my grandmother and children ran. My grandfather entrusted my father with managing all the family's financial affairs and appointed him trustee of his assets.

My father was a very hard worker. Even though he spent much of his time in the store, he managed to be an excellent student and athlete. He participated in tennis, horseback riding, golf, and swimming.

When my father was able to drive, he would take the family on Sundays to Pointe Pelee in Leamington, Canada after closing the store. Each week, the family celebrated with a picnic lunch of homemade grape leaves or stuffed zucchini (cusa) and by swimming in the lake until dusk.

After attending a few years of college, my father came to the United States to work for Ollie Samhat in his large, successful grocery store on Peterborough Avenue in downtown Detroit. It stayed open until 2 a.m, and my father worked the night shift. Ollie loved my father and introduced him to Virginia, his daughter. He became a naturalized citizen and married Virginia in 1938.

In 1955, Ollie Samhat passed away. My father decided to pursue his dream and opened one of the first businesses in Oak Park, Ernie's Neighborhood Market, with his wife Virginia and son Ernie, age nine, at his side. Many frequented the market. He was an excellent butcher and always believed in having quality meat and groceries for his customers. His motto was "Only the Best for You."

My father was a very generous man. He often extended credit to those who did not have money for milk and bread and other necessities. My father wrote the charges on an index card and put them in a little box that is still in the store today. Many old customers come back to see if their names are in the box. One man recently paid his dad's bill for $2.50.

Many customers visited to chitchat every day. Sometimes they would buy something, sometimes they would not. A visit to my father's business brought a smile to everyone's face. He always had a new story to tell.

My father was a very proud man. From his meager origins, he worked hard to provide the best for his family, working seven days a week with his wife and son at his side until his wife became ill in 1969. Then, he and I ran the store.

One day, he drove by the General Motors Building and saw a beautiful white convertible in the window. Lois, his oldest daughter, was not quite sixteen. That Christmas in 1957, Lois, fifteen, and me, fourteen, found the Impala convertible in the garage on Christmas morning. In 1961, he brought home an Oldsmobile for me to drive back and forth to work. But Lois took it out and smashed the passenger side. She was so worried she would get scolded that she had me take it to the repair shop every day and bring it home every night to be parked in the garage, so my father would not see the dent.

Because of his work at the store, my father had an active social life and had many friends. He was an active member of the Masons, the largest and oldest fraternity in the world, and was a faithful Muslim. Generous to a fault, he would give anyone the shirt off his back. Once he even gave one of the customers the family fan. He never heard the end of it from his wife. In 1991, my father died suddenly from a brain aneurysm. He was 79 and worked up to the last day of his life.

I took over the store and ran it as my father had, but times changed, and it became harder to make a living in a little corner market. People went to A&P, Farmer Jack, and Great Scott, but I tried not to let it bother me. Like all the years before, I got up every day, seven days a week and managed the store from 8:30 a.m. to 9:00 p.m. and Sundays from 11:00 a.m. to 2:00 p.m.

In the beginning I made sandwiches the way my father did. I used two slices of Wonder Bread, a thin slice of cheese, a tomato so thin you could see through it, a piece of ham, and a lettuce leaf. I sold them to school kids and workmen. I made them in the morning and put them on the counter. Because I was the only employee, I used the honor system. Customers would take a sandwich and leave their money in the box.

Like my father, I loved Oak Park. My customers were part of my family and a big part of my life. I am dedicated to the community being recognized as "Oak Park's Good Will Ambassador." I too, am generous and believe that my customers deserve nothing but the best. If they needed a toilet snake, I supplied it, a pair of crutches, heat gun, plunger—I had those too. If I didn't have something, I would get it. One day a man walked in with his children and told me that he used to come to the store with his grandma as a boy. However, his parents divorced, and he lost track of his mom and grandma. He asked me if I knew where she was. I said, "Come back tomorrow. I will see what I can do." The next day he came back, and I gave him his grandma's address on Harsen's Island about an hour and a half away. The young man took his family to meet his grandma, and they all flew to California to see his mom. They sent me a picture of the family together with a "thank you" note. The following year the mom, grandma, young man, and his children visited my market to thank me in person.

During the recession, people needed to eat, and many were struggling. So, I started making bigger sandwiches. I was famous for my $ 5.00 sandwich known as the Ernie Burger or Ernie Club. This was when I started saying "Love You, Baby." I wanted people to know I cared, but I could not remember everyone's name, so I started calling everyone "Baby." I felt that everyone is a "baby" to someone. Over the years my sandwiches had grown bigger and bigger. Today, I am famous for the Ernie Monster: seven different meats, two different cheeses, and lots and lots of vegetables topped with mustard, mayo, and Ernie's special "Love Spice." Love Spice is my own concoction of spices that puts "magic" in my sandwiches.

Over the years, I have received many awards, both local and national recognition, for admirable customer service and appetizing sandwiches. Ernie's Market has been honored for "The Best Sandwich," "The Best Sandwich Shop," and "The Happiest Sandwich Shop in Michigan." I believe if customers can spend their money with me after working all week, the least I can do is say "thank you" with a good sandwich and a smile. Today, I, Ernie II, insist on staying at the corner of the 100-year-old store that my father, Ernie I, built. I will work with my team to add to the diversity of this country and to make it a better place. I'm honoring my ancestors and my father, who live through me. Every immigrant has a motto and mine is "Only the Best for You." Ernie I and Ernie II are truly earnest!

Connie Miller Hines

I RECALL BEING MESMERIZED at age five by my maternal grandfather's stories of his younger years in America. His parents migrated from Posen, Germany in 1870, seeking the opportunity to settle their own plot of land in Wisconsin. Thus, my grandfather Leo Kakuschke, born in 1886, became a first-generation American.

Homesteading in the 1800s was far from easy for a family with twelve children, so as a teen my grandfather was encouraged to forge his own way. He migrated to an undeveloped part of North Dakota, where, with no means of building a wooden house, he built what they called a sod shanty. There he befriended the Dakota Sioux Indians, and described helping them find water by using a divining rod and smoking the "peace pipe" around the fire.

Eventually, he moved nearby to the small town of Shields, North Dakota and married my grandmother, Mable Cannons. In 1917 he joined the Navy to help fight for his country in World War I, and was stationed at the Aeronautical Station in Pensacola, Florida. It was there he saw an airplane for the first time.

Heartache and loss came in 1918 when his son Victor died at age four during the influenza epidemic. The epidemic spread fast and killed an estimated 50 million people worldwide that year. Although I was young when hearing him tell the story, his words are still embedded in my memory: "Losing a child takes a piece of your soul."

A second generation was soon to follow. My mother Viola was born in 1920 in the backroom of a cabin at Pelican Lake, Minnesota. This generation was to experience the Great Depression in 1929, and the family lost the house in Fargo, North Dakota that my

Connie Miller Hines *is a thirty-five-year dedicated educator and school administrator. Beyond the classroom she founded numerous Student Assistance Programs to address students' needs, teach equality, and bring harmony to communities. Among her many recognitions she is proud to have received the distinguished Indiana Peacemaker Award. She is retired and resides in Canadian Lakes, Michigan. The photo is of Connie at age 16.*

grandfather had built himself. The only place they could afford to live was in a room in a basement with a hole in the floor for a toilet. Work could not be found so my grandfather joined the federal program called the Civilian Conservation Corps and was assigned to a camp in South Dakota. He tells of making a meager $30 a month, which he sent home to the family. Fortunately, it was there that he furthered his carpentry skills, and later utilized his skills the remainder of his life to provide for his family.

I marvel at what his life in America encompassed, from living in a sod shanty among the Dakota Sioux to seeing American astronauts walk on the moon in 1969. Prior to his passing in 1986, he entrusted to me a small tin box, and perhaps the cherished contents best depict his 96 years as a first-generation American. Upon opening it I held in my hand a tintype photo of his immigrant parents, an Indian arrowhead, an American flag when it only had 48 stars, and a tattered pocket Bible which on the front page he had written **Proud American Leo Kakuschke.**

ॐ ✿ ॐ

My Fraternal American Immigrants
Connie Hines Seventh Generation

I did not explore my father's ancestral American immigrants until recently, and as I write this, I am 72 years of age. My father Merlin Miller was the registrar at the University of Michigan until his death at age 49. I often wish that I could have known him in my adult years. I knew his family were Mormons who lived in Utah, and that my father had departed from the Mormon Church in his early twenties. I was raised attending the Congregational Church on the University of Michigan campus in Ann Arbor, Michigan, where I taught Sunday school and later married. Only recently did I discover that coincidentally my eighth great grandfather was a Congregational reverend in the American colonies.

I was astonished to discover that my father's American heritage went back 380 years. Abraham Pierson, my eighth great grandfather, sailed to the New World in 1639. He was a Puritan born in Yorkshire, England and came to America seeking religious freedom. Shortly after

A young Leo Kakuschke *at age 20, taken in 1906.*

his arrival in 1640, he helped establish Southampton, a colony on Long Island. In 1646, Abraham had a son Abraham Pierson III, and he too would make his mark on American history. He was an early student at Harvard and became a Congregational minister in Newark, New Jersey. Later he assumed the pulpit in Killingsworth, Connecticut in 1694. It was there he helped establish Yale, the third college in America and resided as the first president of Yale until his death in 1707. His statue stands at Yale today.

The Pierson generations to follow resided in Killingsworth until 1842, when Harmon Pierson converted to the LDS Mormon religion. He fled west by wagon train because of religious persecution for the practice of polygamy. Settling in Willard, Utah he built each of his three wives a house and had 31 children. (The practice of polygamy was outlawed in 1890 by the federal government; the Mormon Church discontinued polygamy over a century ago, and since then, excommunicates anyone who practices it.) Harmon contributed to America by helping build the railroads. In 1869 he saw the Union Pacific and the Central Pacific Railroads joined together to unite the East and West coasts, which forever changed travel in America. The government erected a monument at his grave honoring him for his contribution to the building of America.

All immigrants to America, whether in centuries past or recently, bring their values, traditions, and beliefs from their families and countries of origin. All contribute to the collage that makes America unique, beautiful, and forever changing. As an educator for over thirty years I am proud to be a descendant of those who, with the dream of freedom, understood that education will enlighten, unite, and bring growth to America. Finally, after viewing our ancestors' lives, let's flip the switch and pose this question: If your ancestors could see you now, would they be proud?

Sahar Khaldi *has a bachelor's degree in business administration, and she has been working as an accountant for several years. She lives in Dearborn with her husband. She is very active in the community as well with the Michigan Democratic Party. She has been a member of the Dearborn Democratic Club and the 12th Congressional District for several years. She has been elected precinct delegate for two terms. She loves outdoor activities and enjoys traveling.*

Sahar Khaldi

AS A YOUTH, I always dreamed of coming to America. I am Palestinian, but my parents brought me up in Kuwait and then moved to Jordan. My parents suggest that I marry my cousin. I was 20 years old. I told them, "I will do whatever you suggest." In the course of one year of engagement, we spoke frequently over the phone, although the conversations would last a maximum of five minutes. So, we married, not really knowing one another. We lived in Palestine and had three children together but then divorced.

My brother suggested that I move to Jordan, which I did. I could not bring my children from Palestine to Jordan. I worked for a professional consulting group there. My mom and stepfather were living in Kentucky and suggested that I move there, which I did. My former in-laws were raising my children in Palestine.

My family was involved in a lot of businesses in Louisville, Kentucky. My knowledge of the United States was limited to what I had seen on television. When I moved to Kentucky, I didn't see the action that I had seen in American movies and was disappointed! There was no Lassie. There was no Baywatch or Tarzan! In the beginning, I was confused about adapting to the American lifestyle. I found the language to be difficult. I was not planning to stay for more than a short period of time.

And, after my divorce, I was totally independent.

My brother hired me to work in his convenience store. My job was to be his accountant. I might work two hours a day, but he paid me $200 per week. He told me to go home when I got tired. I had only earned $300 per month in Jordan. I thought I had died and had gone to heaven! I became manager of the store but found it difficult to work with my family. At the same time, I attended Jefferson County Community College and studied radiology. I met Sami Khaldi, who was to become my husband, and moved to Michigan.

I then attended Henry Ford College and got a degree in business administration followed by a bachelor's degree from Sienna Heights University. I got a job working in accounting and decided to return to Henry Ford College and study accounting.

The relationship with my children has been difficult. While I spoke with them frequently over the phone, I was not close to them. However, I recently returned to Palestine and re-established my relationship. We now are on better terms, even though my children do not call me "mom."

I am now an American citizen. When I lived in Kentucky, I belonged to a peace community. In Michigan, I belong to the Dearborn Democratic Club, the 12th Congressional District and the Michigan Democratic Party. I am the treasurer of the Federal Bureau of Investigation's Citizen Academy Detroit Chapter organization. Interestingly, when I returned to Palestine, everyone said they knew I was American by the way I carried myself.

I would like my children to move to the United States, but I have told them that in the United States there is no social life, only work life.

Of the differences I have found in the United States it is not difficult to say, "I am sorry." That is not true in the Middle East.

I am now an American. I like it here. I am very proud to be American. For that I am not sorry!

Sami Khaldi

I DID WELL IN SCHOOL in my native country, Jordan, and I had the highest scores on my college entrance exam. I originally enrolled in medical school; however, I switched majors, and earned a bachelor's degree in civil engineering from the University of Jordan. My dream was to advance myself and immigrate to the United States, the land of opportunity.

I wanted to immigrate not only for economic opportunities, but also to exercise my basic human rights and freedom of speech. The United States is a country that recognizes human values and a nation that reaches out to other nations when people suffer from national disasters.

I arrived in America in 1991 on a student visa. While my classes in engineering were taught in American English, I yearned to improve my language skills. I enrolled at St. Clair County Community College and Baker College in Port Huron, Michigan. At the same time, I enrolled in a language class at the school district's continuing education program.

I wanted to improve my American English as fast as I could to make a living and to attend an American university. I took a job at a restaurant with the hope that my daily interactions with customers would help expedite my mission. I was part of the managerial staff. I worked in both the kitchen and the dining room.

The transition from Jordan to the United States was difficult since learning a second language is not always easy, but I managed to excel. I made friends with a Hungarian barber who not only helped me assimilate into the culture but helped other foreign students as well.

Sami Khaldi *is a registered professional engineer (1997) with a master's degree, a licensed realtor (2003), and has been working for Wayne County, Michigan for many years. He is the first Arab American to be the president of the Dearborn Democratic Club. He has been a precinct delegate for five terms and a state central committee member for three terms. Sami was a delegate for presidential candidate Hillary Clinton in 2016 and now he is a delegate for presidential candidate Joe Biden. Sami loves outdoor activities and farming. He is pictured with his wife, Sahar, above.*

I married and had three beautiful children Sharee, Sathe, and Sariyah. Sharee graduated with honors from Eastern Michigan University as a Business Administration major. Sathe graduated with an honors degree from the University of Michigan-Dearborn and is now enrolled at Wayne State University's law school, and Sariyah is studying sports management at Oakland University.

I married my current wife, Sahar Khaldi, in 2013. We are happily married. Throughout my professional life, I have been working as a civil engineer in different capacities. I obtained my master's degree in civil engineering from the University of Detroit Mercy. While I worked for private companies initially, I now work for the Wayne County Department of Public Services in the engineering field. I started at the lowest level—Highway Technician—and am currently an Engineer 7, which is the highest level in the civil service structure. Since 2018, I have been the head of the Testing and Inspection Office.

I have become involved in politics. I have learned that you can either sit at the table or be part of the menu. I prefer to be at the table. It is good to be able to help make decisions that affect your future. I belong to the Dearborn Democratic Club, have held various offices and am now the longest serving president of the organization. I am serving my fifth term as precinct delegate. I am on the executive board of the 12th Congressional District, and a delegate at the state central committee. I am the recording secretary of the Michigan Democratic Party. I was a delegate representing Hilary Clinton at the 2016 Democratic National Convention.

As an immigrant, I am able to communicate with my friends in Jordan and explain that the actions of President Trump do not reflect the feelings and philosophy of most Americans. I find it meaningful to give back to my community. I am a member of the Sheriff Department's Community Emergency Response Team reserve. My family includes not only my wife and blood relatives but also the many friends that I have amassed in the United States, especially those who belong to the Democratic Party. I am proud to be an American.

Olga Klekner is an award-winning, bilingual poet, published both in Hungarian and English. Her essays and poetry have appeared in literary journals and anthologies in the United States and Canada. Her poetry has been 'translated' to canvas by American and Canadian artists and performed on stage by actors. She is a member of Springfed Arts and the Academy of American Poets.

The photo is of Olga at age 4 in her native country in the small city of Vásárosnamény, at that time part of Communist Hungary of 1956. A few months later Russian tanks rumbled through her small city on their way to Budapest to suppress the Hungarian revolution. Olga remembers "standing at the gate, feeling the earth roar under me."

Olga Klekner

WE ALL LIVE on Sagan's "pale blue dot," a planet with a history of borders, augmented territories, bullied countries. The world is rarely unbroken somewhere, and old ideas for a new life are brought to the United States from every corner of the world. This is where we wish to save the integrity of mankind, where we want to save one another, where our best hope for a life lived in freedom has the best chance to become reality.

I had no intention to move to the United States from Hungary, but hearts have been known to run off with their youthful agendas. I met my future husband, a US citizen, in 1971 and married him two years later. It was difficult to become an immigrant, to leave my family and enter a new country, learn a new language, and get to know my husband's family. My father-in-law and his wife were refugees, part of a political migration that took place after World War II. For them, the push-factor was war, the threat of ensuing persecution.

In the 1940s during World War II, suspecting a sweeping Soviet occupation, my in-laws and thousands of others fled Hungary and spent four years in an overcrowded camp for refugees in Austria. My husband was born in a cloister during those unpredictable, anxiety-ridden years. Speaking perfect French and several other languages, my father-in-law was offered a position in France, but his determined destination was the New World with all its legendary opportunities. The family arrived in New York into a cautiously welcoming atmosphere: they were citizens of a defeated enemy. My father-in-law's military academy and law degree were worthless in the States. He lost his influential position in society, even his full name. His side of the Klekner family comes from nobility, and the hereditary surname-title given by Emperor Franz Joseph could not be used in the United States.

Imagine a young woman entering this family at the age of 21 who grew up with socialist ideology, whose father was a colonel in Hungary's socialist army, whose paternal grandparents raised nine children in a thatch-roofed house. Here, I was introduced to my new family's circle of immigrant friends, some of them aristocrats who were forced to leave everything behind in a country struggling to find its identity under the Soviet Union's political directive. Many who stayed behind were proclaimed to be the enemy of the people. Their homes were confiscated, some were forced to enter labor camps; others simply perished. Back home, I caught threads of whispers about political prisoners. In Detroit, I befriended Antal Koosa, a poet, who with his writer wife Maria were beaten so severely in a Hungarian jail back in the unforgiving politics of the 1950s that she lost her pregnancy. They were freed during the short-lived success of revolutionary forces in 1956 and later welcomed in the States. Maria worked for a social agency, and on weekends she visited old women in nursing homes. She gifted them with small bottles of cologne. "I want them to feel that they are still ladies," she would say.

Living in America alters us profoundly. This is the country that offers wings with citizenship. While studying for a degree in psychology, I fell in love with the English language, wrote a column for the student paper and began writing creatively, later publishing my poetry. I was a volunteer probation officer for years, donated my sculpted wearable artworks to charity, and exhibited my photographs. I now help count raptors and passerines for a migration observatory, and since they have become endangered species, I raise monarch butterflies in my delightful journey of discovery. I owe this country my torn-down walls.

Other than Native Americans, we are all immigrants or descendants of immigrants. We rise at dawn to bake fresh bread, and at night we patrol the streets for safety. We worship in our homes, churches, mosques, and synagogues. We are presidents and first ladies. We are heart surgeons, nurses, teachers, and astronauts that soar to the moon. Some of us are billionaires while others work three jobs to pay for their livelihood. We are Blue Star families, Supreme Court judges, and senators. We are Wall Street and we occupy Wall Street. We are poets and writers. We wrote the Constitution and the National Anthem. "We're the nation that just had six of our scientists and researchers win Nobel Prizes," the White House tweeted in 2016, "and every one of them was an immigrant."

We are the open heart of the world. We honor one another's cultures and share exciting culinary delights. We celebrate Chinese New Year, Cinco de Mayo, Paczki Day, St Patrick's Day, Christmas, Hanukah, Kwanzaa, and Ramadan.

There are people in broken countries whose whispers spell burden and hardship. They dream of leaving behind missing skies, and homes with bullet-riddled walls. They sit among ashes that hold the memory of flames.

May America allow them the astonishing gift of belonging.

Victoria Kolias *was born in San José, Costa Rica. She immigrated to the United States in 1964 where she graduated from Wayne State University with a bachelor's degree in Spanish and French. She earned a master's degree in Bicultural Education in Spanish and English. She taught for 20 years in the high schools and four years at Henry Ford College in Dearborn. Vickie is currently retired and resides in Rochester Hills, Mich. She spends her winter months in Clearwater, Florida.*

Victoria Paspalis Kolias

WITH THE ENDLESS political, economic, and military corruption in Greece after World War II, my father, Epaminondas Paspalis, left Theba, Greece in 1939. He was in his late 20s and in search of a better life. His desire was to emigrate to Chile, and to become wealthy. He was accompanied by four other Greek nationals who shared in his dream. With the encouragement of the Greek government, these young men boarded the ship in hope of gaining employment or to develop permanent business establishments. While en route, the ship stopped in Costa Rica. The captain told his passengers that they had arrived and that this was his last stop. Once on land, my father and his friends realized they were not in Chile—they were in Costa Rica. They did not have much choice but to explore the country and decide whether to stay or take another ship to Chile. My father sensed comfort in the new land and decided to stay. He found work almost immediately. He later met my mother, married, and started a family. Costa Rica became his permanent residence. As they say, "Your country is where you live."

I was born in 1942 in San Jose, Costa Rica. My mother was born and raised in Costa Rica. She was of Spanish descent. My parents led a happy life until my father passed away in an accident at the age of 33. My mother was young and left to care for two children without a source of revenue. My brother was two years old, and I was three months old. She did not have a formal education, nor the business skills required to secure an income for her family. She was not well emotionally and in no time exhausted everything my father had left her. She was forced to move in with my uncle, my aunt, and their four children. We became part of an extended family. We lived comfortably in the beginning. My aunt and uncle treated us as they did their own children. My cousins and I treated one another like brothers and sisters. However, my uncle was a disciplinarian, and my aunt had a strong personality. She was very controlling. My mother did not have much of a say in anything. My aunt told her, "Either you or I will raise the children." My aunt took charge.

My father's death and the harsh circumstances that my mother endured led to a deep depression. My aunt sent her to Mexico for treatment. At the time, Mexico was more advanced in mental health concerns than Costa Rica. I do not believe my aunt wanted my mother to return to Costa Rica since she never sent her a plane ticket. My mother's legal documents had expired, and she remained in Mexico. She survived with the small income she received monthly from my aunt. My brother and I had inherited my parents' home. My aunt rented it out and sent the money to my mother. Twenty years later, my cousin and her husband decided to bring my mother back to Costa Rica, but by then my brother and I had immigrated to the United States. Essentially, we grew up without a mother or father. During the years that we lived with my aunt and uncle, we experienced intense anxiety, my brother especially. He had heaps of repressed anger because we were left in the dark about my mother's condition. It was hard to grow up and not know why we had lost our mother. I found relief in school and with my teachers and friends. I yearned for an education and enjoyed going to school. Temperamentally, I was the opposite of my brother.

My uncle and aunt sent all their children to college in the United States. They wanted them to have a quality education that they could not obtain in Costa Rica. Since I lived in the same household, once I finished high school, I too, immigrated to United States. In 1963, I entered the US with a green card because I met the immigration requirements. My goal was to go to school. I had all my legal documents and a US sponsor. My sponsor was my other cousin who was already an American citizen and worked at Harper Hospital in Detroit. She was also working on her Ph.D. in microbiology while teaching at Wayne State University School of Medicine. I lived with her for a year at her home in Detroit, close to the Wayne State University campus.

Eventually, I moved into a dormitory at WSU and worked for the Spanish department in the School of Education. My friends and social life were mainly on campus. I belonged to Wayne State's Latin America and (Delphi) Greek clubs. I participated in programs on campus and attended events in all clubs. My future husband also belonged to the Delphi Club. He and his family had immigrated to the US during the civil war in Greece.

When I began my education at Wayne State University in fall 1963, I scored very low on my English entrance exam because I did not know how to speak, read, or write in English. It was a university requirement for non-English speakers to pass two semesters of English before enrolling in Freshmen English. Initially, I wanted to major in medical technology. I signed up for classes, but my weakness in the English language became a barrier. I then decided to change my major from medical technology to teaching. I worked on a Spanish major and a French minor. After a great deal of hard work and struggle, I graduated in 1967. I married my husband the same year. He too, had graduated, with a master's in Electrical Engineering. He took a job with Chrysler Defense.

My first teaching job was shortly after the riots in Detroit. I worked at MacFarlane Junior High. I didn't have teaching experience and working with teenagers was a challenge. Some students were bitter and difficult, and my first year was a learning experience. On the bright side, I learned a lot about Detroit's Black history and culture, a very different history than Blacks in South and Central America.

I did not return to teaching the following year because I was pregnant. After the birth of my daughter, I returned to WSU to study two years of modern Greek. I obtained a Permanent Teaching Certificate and became fluent in the Greek language. Subsequently, I had two more daughters but continued to take graduate classes.

I earned a master's degree in Bilingual Education, Spanish and English. I worked in two different private Catholic schools. I taught Spanish and French at St. Mary of Redford in Detroit, and at Aquinas High School in Southgate. I was also occasionally a substitute teacher in Detroit and the Dearborn Public Schools and taught mainly Spanish, French, and English as a Second Language (ESL). I was hired full-time at Dearborn High School where I taught Spanish language and culture, and some French for over twenty years. I took students on trips to Spain, Mexico and France. I also did several cultural programs in Spanish. I retired from Dearborn schools in 2006, but I continued to substitute teach. I was also an adjunct instructor at Henry Ford College in Dearborn for four years, where I taught Spanish. My teaching experience at the college was rewarding, and I fully retired in 2016.

Today, I enjoy my home in Rochester Hills along with my husband, my grandchildren, and the rest of the family. I also enjoy traveling during the harsh winter months we endure in Michigan to spend time at our condo in Clearwater, Florida.

I am grateful to have had the opportunity to immigrate to the US. This country offered me many educational and employment opportunities I may never have had if I remained in Costa Rica. My life in this country has been fulfilling. I feel fortunate to have a pension and health benefits and equally fortunate to have raised three beautiful daughters and offered them a quality education. This country is a multicultural society, and its stream of immigrants has given it a colorful texture and an inspiring narrative. I have learned to appreciate different languages and cultures. To appreciate and understand immigrants, it is crucial to have shared in their experience—which I have. My immigration experience has made me more understanding toward other immigrants and their needs.

I achieved the American dream. I am grateful. God bless America—the land of opportunity.

Samir Leon

I CAME TO THE UNITED STATES from Syria as an engineering student in 1977. I began my studies at Oakland Community College in Michigan and took a job washing dishes at the Big Boy restaurant. One day, early in my employment, I could not get my car into "drive." I drove to the restaurant in reverse—for seven miles!

After two years, I became a cook and forgot about engineering. By 1983, my brothers, Walid and Moulid, and I saved up enough money for a down payment on a restaurant in Novi. In 1986 we started another restaurant in Livonia.

In 1987 we opened Leon's in Dearborn. We had three bad years. In 1990 we almost lost the business. My wife, who is a very religious person, had a dream that we should restructure our building. We all agreed to go ahead with her plan. We put $30,000 into renovations, and we never looked back.

We began to host free Thanksgiving dinners in 1991. We decided to make this a tradition for as long as we were in business. My employees donate their time. I figure that we have given out at least 17,000 dinners. I believe in giving back to the community. Some people leave tips, which we give to charities. I estimate that we have given away $80,000 through the years.

We have had up to 12 restaurants at one time but now have eight. I think that we are successful because we work hard. I work at least ten hours but usually 14 hours per day, seven days a week. We have good help. Six employees have been with me between 19 and 22

Samir Leon *lives with his wife and daughter in Plymouth, Michigan. Samir communicates regularly with his sister in Syria. His business has survived the COVID 19 virus with the help of loyal customers who have made use of his carry-out service.*

years. They are like family. Whenever they need help, I give it to them. We take care of our customers. The customer is always right.

We use 180 dozen eggs each day during the week and 360 dozen on Saturday and Sunday. We use 80 pounds of coffee a day. We make our own hash brown potatoes and use 1,200 pounds a week.

I was close friends with Mayor Guido. One day he wanted me to go to an event, and I was running late. He took me to his home and outfitted me in his clothes. Then we went off together. I went with Mr. Guido to the US Conference of Mayors in 2006. Through him I saw President Clinton three times. I was also "adopted" by John Nichols, the former Oakland County executive.

I still have family in Syria. I call home and talk for about 25 minutes every day.

God bless America. It is truly a land of opportunity. My family came from Syria with nothing and now look at us!

This story was originally published in *Best Dearborn Stories: Voices from Henry Ford's Hometown (Volume III)*.

Dr. Mahnaz Mafee *is a board-certified Nurse Practitioner. In addition to her doctorate degree, she holds a master's degree as an adult nurse practitioner and another master's in gerontology. She works with geriatric patients and treats allergy patients because her Ph.D is in Biology with a concentration in Immunology-Allergy.*

Dr. Mahnaz Mafee

EQUALITY IS WHAT MOST PEOPLE SEEK, but some of us feel we deserve to be placed on a pedestal. To explain my comment, I will begin by sharing my background and life history. I was born in Iran. I finished high school, married, and immigrated to the United States of America 50 years ago.

My appreciation of all religions was passed down to me either through genetics or the behavioral modeling I observed as a young girl in Iran. My great-grandfather, my grandfather, and uncles were all historians. My grandfather wrote a notable book on the history of Jesus. Although my family was not overly orthodox, they still believed in and practiced Islam.

As a child, my nanny took me to the mosque every afternoon for prayer. After she died and as I grew older and went to high school, religious practice changed in my life. We lived in the suburbs of Tehran, Iran's capital, but I went to school in the city. It was customary then for students to go home between 12 p.m. and 2 p.m. to eat lunch and rest, and then return to school afterward.

My home was too far from school, so I stayed behind for the two-hour break. In a way, I had the freedom to do anything I wanted. My parents trusted me and had given me permission to leave the school with some of my friends. My classmates were all Iranians who practiced different religions; I had Christian, Jewish, Baha'i and Zoroastrian friends. I was very sociable and became very close to my friends—to a point that I would attend their church services and learn about their religious practices during lunch breaks.

On Sundays, I attended Catholic Mass with my friends. I became fascinated by Catholicism; I even volunteered in the church kitchen to help the nuns. My parents were not aware of my interaction and fascination with Catholicism. My fascination was so strong that I decided to become a nun. I was nearly 15 years old at the time. When I shared my ideas with my parents, they did not verbally object, but they privately mapped out my marital plans. Soon after, I met with a suitor at the door of my home. He was Muslim and a physician; I was barely 16, and now, 50 years later, we are happily married.

We came to America so my husband could advance his career, and I could go to college. We studied hard, worked long hours, paid our taxes, supported our families here and overseas but did not fail to notice the lack of equality we faced in America. I remember several incidents where I was not treated fairly. I had to work harder and earn good grades to receive the same treatment from my instructors at the universities I attended. I found myself continuously negotiating with my employers to receive a raise or a position that fit my education level and achievements. Although I had two doctoral degrees, I did not receive what I believe was the respect I deserved.

This lack of fairness was more evident coming from Caucasian employers and instructors and at times African Americans as well. I felt like some African Americans projected the pressures of racist backlash they experienced onto foreigners. Some seemed to think foreigners came to the United States to steal their jobs. It appeared that many of the immigrants I encountered had a higher education than the average American, and these same immigrants worked harder and spent longer hours at their jobs to earn their living. They had no choice; this was the only way to survive in this new land—the land of opportunity.

I recall that when I tried to transfer to a pharmacy program in Michigan before I even took my seat in the classroom in 1974, the Dean of the Pharmacy school loudly stated: "What are you doing here? We don't have any room for you!" I needed only 17 credits to graduate from pharmacy school.

During the Iran hostage crisis, I experienced racism and hate from my neighbors when they sent their dog to chase me. I experienced inequality when I applied to join the audiology program. For them to accept me, I was sent to a speech pathologist at St. Joseph's Hospital to improve my English. After nine months of hard work and practice, I gave up.

I also experienced prejudice in the '80s when my foreign classmate and I applied to the field of medical technology to learn how to work with robots in the lab. We were the only two candidates out of hundreds who were rejected. We both had the necessary prerequisites. I even had a Ph.D., but that wasn't enough. Eventually, I followed my passion. I wanted to help needy people. This was something that I had always wanted to do. It was one of the reasons I wanted to become a Catholic nun when I was young. I was determined to become a nurse. After years of education and accomplishments, I was the last one to be accepted into the program.

After 9/11, hatred toward Muslims has been on the rise. Today many Americans display negative sentiments toward immigrants. This is noticeable among all classes in American society. Hate that is harbored against immigrants extends to anyone who does not look American or does not practice Christianity. Ironically, the Christianity that I was familiar with did not advocate hate, racism or prejudice. When did Jesus ever mention that one group, one creed, or one nation was better than another?

Sadly, my experience of prejudice in the school system and workplace took away my happiness. When I look back on my life, I see 30 years spent in school, in the classroom and the library. When did I have time to enjoy my children? When did I enjoy living? When did I have time to benefit from one field, serve society, and build a safe nest for my retirement?

We should be ashamed of ourselves for allowing the hate that exists in the White House to spread across the country. How will we explain this to the Almighty God? Will He not be unhappy about the abuses and prejudice in the world today? Is there a solution?

By sharing bits and pieces of my own experience as a foreigner and a Muslim, I hope readers realize how difficult it is to live in this society and be accepted by Americans. I hope this account will bring forth compassion for immigrants and non-Caucasians. However, this is not just a problem for Christians or Americans; all races and religions need to be more accepting of each other. Muslims need to respect non-Muslims, Jews and Christians, Arabs and non-Arabs, and Blacks and Caucasians also need to accept each other to resolve racial issues. The real enemy is hatred and racism amongst mankind; we are all truly equal in the eyes of the Lord.

Shannon Murphy

MY FAMILY'S PATH started in Newfoundland, Canada, its own country at the time. From there they moved to Ontario, Canada. I was born in Windsor, Ontario, but soon after there was a promotion for my father in Pennsylvania, and later, Michigan. I was four years old and have only vague memories of moving to the United States; however, to this day, I recall the excitement of opportunity, the long drive with my three siblings and our belongings packed in our car.

I completed K-12 in the USA, my bachelors at Concordia University in Montreal, and my master's degree in science at Wayne State University in Detroit. Over the years, I maintained my green card and status as permanent resident of the United States. I married Rebecca O'Kray, an American citizen who was in law school at Wayne State University when we met.

Professionally, I have been fortunate to be in the water industry. My career starting at NSF International in Ann Arbor, a company which tests, audits, and certifies water, health science, and consumer products. From there I moved to the manufacturing sector for two companies who manufacture water filtration products. In addition, I have been able to volunteer for our industry association, becoming the president of our state water purification association as well as serving as a regulatory leader and industry lobbyist for safe and affordable drinking water. I am the proud father of three successful children and Scout, our faithful dog.

I am happily married to Rebecca, an attorney licensed in Michigan, Arizona, and California! Reb and

I have a fun—never dull life. She is a vegan Democrat and I am a red meat conservative. We both respect each other's views and discuss topics calmly and logically.

Shannon Murphy *is an American "Newfy" (someone from Newfoundland) who has had his wife and kids kiss both the cod and the Blarney Stone. He is a man of faith. He enjoys his family. He is a water expert, gardener guru, Stand Up Paddle Board and basketball player. He loves dogs and cats.*

I might have remained a green card holding permanent resident had it not been for a quirk of fate. One evening my father-in-law, who is also a veggie Democrat, and I got into a heated political discussion. The discussion ended when he stated, "Shannon, it doesn't matter what you think because you can't vote." I angrily left the room. He apologized, and we reconciled. But that led me to consider becoming an American citizen.

Becoming a US Citizen is expensive, which required taking money out of my savings. I submitted my application for citizenship. This was not easy because my wife is the family finance guru governing the cash flow, and since she had told me what my father-in-law had said, I wanted to keep what I was doing a secret. I did while I studied to for my citizenship test.

One night, I came home from work to surprise Rebecca. I told her we had to have a serious talk. Her face turned ashen. As it turns out, my sock drawer is not a good place to hide money as she had found what I was squirreling away to become a citizen. She wasn't sure if I was going to buy her a major gift, was involved in selling drugs, or planned on running away! Her face brightened when I began, "Remember when I had that tiff with your dad?"

She was relieved and quite happy when I announced my plans for citizenship. I was sworn in as a US Citizen on July 2, 2010. My father-in-law wasn't so pleased. He said, "I can't believe I created a voting Republican!"

This country has provided me with the right to express my political views openly and freely while offering me ample opportunity to progress educationally and financially.

Nancy Owen Nelson *is an English professor with academic book and article publications; recently, she has explored her family history through memoir (*Search for Nannie B. *and soon* Divine Aphasia, *both from Ardent Writer Press) and poetry. Her latest poetry collection is* Portals: A Memoir in Verse *(Kelsay Books, 2019).*

She is pictured here with her father, Woodford Owen Nelson, in 1951.

Dr. Nancy Owen Nelson

I DON'T REALLY have an immigrant story. That is, unless you consider my ancestors who came to this continent, these United States, before the Revolutionary War established our independence from England. John Chandler, my earliest traceable kin on ancestry.com (so far), and my ninth great-grandfather, was born in Wiltshire, England and arrived here sometime after the death of his father Richard in 1620. He married Elizabeth Lupo, and their first child, Richard, was born in Virginia in 1624. There are other early immigrants in my family tree—William Nelson II, my tenth great-grandfather, who came to the Massachusetts Colony sometime between the death of his mother, Margaret Swain Johnson Nelson (1625), and the birth of his son, William Nelson III (1640); William Owen, my eighth great-grandfather, born in Wales in 1673, who came here sometime before the birth of his daughter Susannah Anne, in 1684; and Hans Jacob Russell, my fifth great-great grandfather, who was born in Zurich, Switzerland in 1728 and arrived in Pennsylvania in 1743. These are my four family lines.

Researching my ancestral roots led me to understand that my ancestors came to the pre-Revolutionary colonies long before the Latino, Muslim, Asian, or other immigrants who populate my life: Muslim students I teach or friends with whom I share meals; Latinos or Asians who are a part of my family by marriage, or friends whose ancestors immigrated here in the twentieth century from Eastern Europe, Italy, or other countries.

What does this say about my place in this country? We know that the Scots-Irish and others who settled in the American South helped establish the ethos of an agricultural economy dependent on slave ownership. My DNA test shows that I am 98% European; I have no African blood, which means that my ancestors did not necessarily sexually abuse African slaves. However, did they own them?

When I first began researching my ancestry for my memoir, *Searching for Nannie B: Connecting Three Generations of Southern Women,* I feared that I would discover slave ownership in that terrible and unjust history as a part of my legacy. In reviewing census records from the 1850s, I was relieved to find that my maternal great-grandfather, John R. Russell, listed only white workers. His father, Archibald, also listed family members as laborers. A search of census reports for great-grandfather Francis Chandler showed the same, as did that of Charles Banks A. Owen, my third great-grandfather.

Then I found an 1850 Slave Schedule on a Nelson ancestor's profile. My question had been answered, but not in the way I'd hoped. I expressed my feelings in a poem, "Found on Ancestry.com: Fifteen Slaves," recently published in my chapbook, *My Heart Wears No Colors.* In the poem, I imagine one old slave in his labored fatigue— "body bent from/decades of labor over balls/of white cotton, bright as sunshine." I imagine the despair of a mother whose children will never have freedom, a slave girl who doesn't understand the cruelty of the name "picaninny," which the owners' kids call her. I end the poem wondering about my own part in this sad and loathsome history:

> *how could his blood run through*
> *my veins? How can I, these many*
> *years later, own this truth,*
> *own this inheritance—*
> *blistered by sun, worn by labor,*
> *not free? She's thirty. She's finished,*
> *she thinks, 'cause what else*
> *can be ahead for me? A husband*

*in the fields, six chilluns, some
young and underfoot, two of 'em boys
almost men? Men who will have
their own women, they chilluns
but won't be free of the lash,
the chains?*

***

*My father's
father's
father's
father,
how could his blood run through
my veins? How can I, these many
years later, own this truth,
own this inheritance—
blistered by sun, worn by labor,
not free?*

The ancestors of slaves owned by my family could have come to Virginia as early as 1619 on a Dutch ship as indentured servants, or they may have been bought off of ships from Africa in the 1700s, until (and maybe after, illegally) President Thomas Jefferson's act that prohibited slave importation came into law on January 1, 1808.[1]

Instead of burying myself in a dark history, I choose to live in the present, seeking to study, understand, and write about the motivations of my Confederate ancestors, while not condoning the cause for which they fought. A high school friend from Alabama posted something like this on Facebook the day after the Charlottesville incident in 2017 involving neo-Nazis and white supremacists: "I was at a gym working out with some African-American women. We looked at each other, we grasped hands. I said, 'We must work together.'"

If I have an immigration story, here is its message: We must work together.

---

[1]   "The Abolition of the Slave Trade: The Act of 1807," The Schomberg Center for Research in Black Culture, The New York Public Library, accessed April 28, 2020, http://abolition.nypl.org/essays/us_constitution/5/

Anh Nguyen *has been living with his wife and two children in Dearborn, Michigan for 14 years. He loves and devotes himself to the nurturing of his son and daughter, while caring for this beloved partner and wife. He is intrigued by the outdoors, specifically fishing. He also enjoys reading history. He prefers exercising over laziness and sets himself in a mindset of always being productive.*

Anh is pictured with his wife, Connie, and his two children, Fay and Dan.

Anh Nguyen

I LIVE THE GOOD LIFE in Dearborn, Michigan.

My family had led the good life in Vietnam. We lived four hours from Saigon. That was before the Communists took over. You have to live under Communism to understand it. The rich and powerful got away with anything they wanted. Vietnam was ruled by status and by name.

The Communists had complete control. We were not allowed to practice our religion, Catholicism. Communism was like a government-run mafia. The operatives would change the currency from time to time. After a certain date the money we had was no longer good. We had to trade it in for the newer currency. I assume that this was a way of determining who had sizable assets.

The Communists killed several of my relatives in Vietnam. My grandparents wanted some of the family to leave the country. My parents insisted that they stay and help my grandparents. I left the country with my three aunts and uncle. We were considered to be "boat people." We had to pay to get out of the country. We stayed in a camp in the Philippines for two or three years until our paperwork got processed. We were sponsored by the San Diego Catholic Church and entered the country at Los Angeles. I was born on May 12, 1973 and reached the American shore on January 14, 1981.

My relatives got by with odd jobs in California. I had two paper routes, but I had to give all of my earnings to my aunts and uncle. The Vietnamese Catholic community was very supportive.

In California, I worked putting up road signs. Ultimately, I got a job in a Vietnamese-owned sushi restaurant. I worked seven days a week, but I enjoyed it, so that was OK. That led me to get a job as a chef at the Hyatt Hotel just outside of Los Angeles.

I met my wife, Connie, through a high school friend. We have two children, Fay and Dan. My son has skin problems and other health issues, and we were told that Michigan's climate was better for him. So, we came to Michigan. I worked in the Hyatt Regency in Dearborn before it closed. Then I worked at a restaurant called Crave. I have a consulting business now and advise restauranteurs how to run their operations.

Connie and I want our kids to become good people. They are doing well in school. Our daughter has a 3.5 average. Our son has a 4.0 average. We try to teach by example. You can either make the world better or you can make it worse.

I love the American culture. People here tell the truth. They would rather feel the hurt now than later. I believe that your character is your most important possession. What is important is who we are now, not who we were or who we are going to be. I believe that you should never lie to yourself. You should not let other people define who you are or what you should do.

We enjoy living in Dearborn. The neighbors are friendly, and we take care of each other. I bring in our neighbors' mail when they are on vacation. My son cuts our neighbors' grass. I clean off my neighbors' sidewalk when the snow falls. I especially find it meaningful to assist those who are veterans. They gave a lot for their country.

I look out the window and see an elderly couple walking hand in hand. That's the kind of neighborhood I live in. I love it.

Yassin Osman

I AM FROM CAIRO, EGYPT. I first came to the United States on July 21, 2012 to visit a couple I met while taking a class in Paris, France. I have a bachelor's degree in business and an MBA, and I took one class in Paris, which has had an impact on my life ever since.

After I had been in the United States for ten days, my dad called and told me not to return to our Egyptian home. The Arab Spring had turned the country into chaos. There were killings on the street where I lived. The revolution had destroyed all pretenses of safety. The Muslim Brotherhood at that time had a great deal of influence, and if I returned to my homeland, I could very well have been killed.

My dad suggested that I contact a friend of his who lived in Detroit, Michigan. I would say that his friendship was of limited value. He only helped me out at the time by allowing me to sleep on his floor. Then, he moved me to a house he owned which had neither heat nor running water.

I fell into a state of depression. Then, I met Joann McKay, the sister-in-law of the man with whom I lived. She was an angel in disguise. She took me into her home and treated me like family. I lived with her for a year and a half. She took me to a social worker who directed me to an attorney. I didn't have money at the time, but my friend Joanne paid the attorney's fee of $5,000 for help in seeking asylum. I was able to repay her kindness after I found employment.

Unfortunately, the attorney had a seizure and couldn't accompany me to see an asylum officer in Chicago. My paperwork was deficient. Nevertheless, I

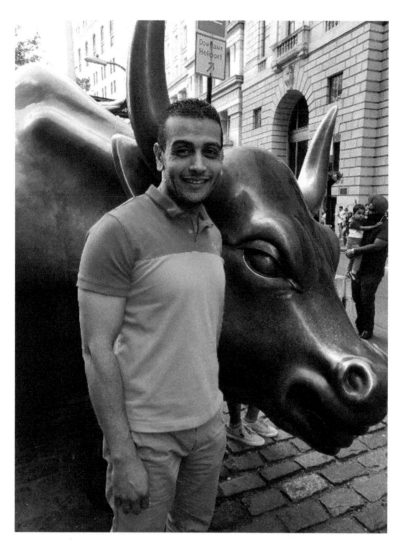

Yassin Osman *is currently working in the Finance Department for the City of Dearborn. He still makes contact through Zoom and visits his American friends, though by phone, because of the COVID 19 virus. He helped gardening and cleaning at the home of his father's friend who passed away so that the family might list their house for sale.*

got a hearing. However, the officer interrogated me for three hours while most of the others in court that day were questioned for 30 minutes. He sent me a letter saying that he could not determine my eligibility for asylum and referred my case to the Immigration and Naturalization Services in Detroit.

Because of the attorney's not having rendered me any service, I asked for a return of my $5,000. After much discussion, I got $1,500 back. I hired another attorney who charged me $3,000. At my next hearing in 2014, she acted like a crazy person. The judge said that if he were to decide on that day, he would have ruled against me. He assigned me a new hearing date in 2016. The attorney was notified of the date but not me. I missed the hearing, and the judge could have deported me. Instead, he assigned me a hearing in 2018.

I hired a new attorney. I paid her $4,000. After she filed paperwork for my application, she dropped me as a client. I asked for at least a partial refund but got none. I was assigned a new hearing date of May 27, 2020. Because of the COVID-19 crisis, the date was changed to April 24, 2023!

Since arriving in the US, I received a work permit. I worked on the assembly line for Ford Motor Company. It paid well. However, the mores of my co-workers left something to be desired. I wanted a professional position. I landed a job working for Fiat-Chrysler Corporation in Auburn Hills, Michigan. The job was taxing. In 2016, I was laid off for 75 days because my work permit had expired, and I didn't receive a new one. At that time the earliest you could apply for a new work permit was three months prior to the expiration date. That's when I applied for the new one, but it usually is delayed for six months. A new software program was introduced in my absence from my job. A woman I worked for seemed to have a chip on her shoulder and was not supportive when I was learning the new system, and that added stress to my job.

Fiat Chrysler had cutbacks in 2018, and I lost my job, which had also paid well. I'd had a good annual review, but that didn't help. I took another job working for the City of Dearborn.

So, I have had a lot of trials and tribulations. In addition to the economic uncertainties, I also felt isolated from other Egyptians. I feel that the only time they contact me is when there is a fundraiser.

I volunteered for the Dearborn Historical Museum. I volunteered in the Spiritual Support Department of Beaumont Hospital. It was a very meaningful experience. A lot of the patients there are Muslims, and I was able to offer them solace in their time of need. I became very close to other volunteers. Jane O'Kray helped me in various ways. Another was "Jimmie" Cheslock, a woman in her nineties, who had to quit as she became frail. I had visited her every Sunday, took her to the Catholic Mass, and had dinner with her. I would then visit Jane and Victor Borowski, a fine couple that I lived with for a while. Unfortunately, "Jimmie" and the Borowskis all died in the last year. So, I have grappled with much sadness while here in the US.

I made friends with many Americans. Most Americans have big hearts. The woman who took me in when I was in dire straits really looked out for me. Her grandchildren refer to me as "Uncle Yassin." I have participated in Christmas activities in a lot of Christian households.

Fearful of being killed, I cannot return to Egypt. Because my status here is so tenuous, I am considering moving to Canada. The Canadian government is looking for people to live and work in rural areas. I really don't want to leave the US. I have met many fine people here. However, I need a green card. I have not seen my parents in eight years. They cannot travel here until I get a green card. I miss them.

Sometimes I feel I must die before anyone notices that I am a good man just trying to lead a normal life.

Diane Palaich-Luxton

I AM CROATIAN, a second-generation Croatian. When I was born, Croatia was part of the Yugoslavian nation, but every Croatian knew Croatia had always been Croatia even though the world knew it as Yugoslavia. When my grandfather, Franjo Palaich, came to the United States, Croatia was then part of the Austria-Hungary nation. Because the Croatian people struggled both politically and economically for centuries and were always governed by other outside forces, they were left with little independent freedom. Beginning in the 1850s, impoverished peasants struggled with infertile soil that rendered very little, along with phylloxera, a vine disease that would eventually ruin the vineyards. Plus, the abolition of the military frontier took away the jobs of those who did not have any other way of support. By the height of the Croatian emigration from 1900 to 1914, 600,000 to 800,000 Croatians permanently immigrated to the United States. Since the majority were poor, illiterate peasants, they believed the earlier immigrant stories sent back to Croatia of the great wealth in America. To come to America, it meant for many the opportunity of good wages and allowed newcomers the freedom of national and religious expression.

My grandfather shared the strong desire of a better life along with his Croatian countrymen, but his story of immigration would not be an easy one. He tried many times over many years to begin his sojourn to America and his determination and hard work would be the turning point of his life story.

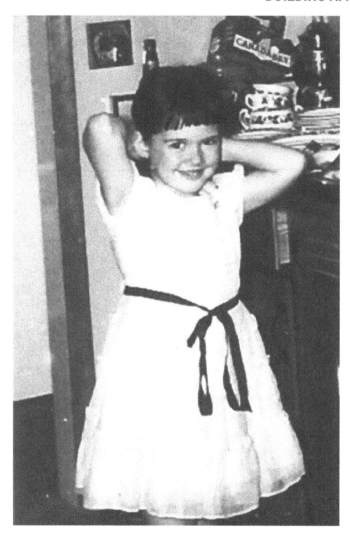

Diane Palaich-Luxton *was raised in a Croatian-Irish family in the Detroit and Cleveland areas. She married Jim Luxton in 1971, raised two sons, and went back to school. She graduated from Wayne State University with a Bachelor's in Education in 1989 and a Master of Social Work in 2000. She's a writer and a publisher. She published* Franjo and Ljubica *in 2014. She currently lives in Arizona with her husband of 50 years.*

The photograph is of Diane as a young girl in 1955.

(Above) Franjo in his butcher shop in Detroit; (Below) Franjo and his wife, Violet, and two daughters, Ann and Rose, in the grocery market portion of one of his two stores. Both photos circa 1922.

Franjo came to the United States, landing at Ellis Island en route to Detroit, Michigan, on October 9, 1905, at the age of 18. Upon landing at Ellis Island, all immigrants were examined by physicians before being allowed into the country. It was after going through a very painful examination—having his eyelids turned inside out— that Franjo and his father, Antun, were denied entrance due to an eye disease called trachoma. Later, I learned, officials looked for trachoma because of the large number of Europeans emigrating with TB, and it was feared that trachoma was a symptom of the contagious disease.

My grandfather was determined that he was not going to give in that easily. After returning to Croatia, he would spend three months in Zagreb receiving treatment for his eye disease. Unable to be totally cured of trachoma, he decided that he would go to South America and from there would board a ship for the US. But once he arrived in South America, he was unable to leave and was detained for nine months. Still determined to immigrate to the United States, Franjo found employment on an American sailboat named the *Snowdon*, which was leaving South America to sail to the United States. Four months later, the ship reached Boston. Upon landing, when asked by the officers if he was going to stay or continue on another ship, Grandpa, afraid of being turned down again because of his eyes, lied to the men in charge, telling them that he was going to move on; but, instead of leaving on the same ship on which he arrived, Franjo traveled on to Detroit by train.

Discovering that life in America would be difficult for him without a trade, Franjo left Detroit once again and returned home to Croatia to study a trade. Even though he knew of the difficulties he would face once he tried to reenter the United States, he was intelligent enough to know that he had to stand out among the thousands of immigrants arriving in United States each day. At the famous Gavrilovic Meat Factory in Petrinja, Croatia, grandpa studied for two years and became a butcher. Now, feeling he could provide for himself, he prepared for another immigration attempt. This time, equipped with a trade and the courage to face another border crossing, he sailed from Havre, France on the ship *Sardinian* bound for Canada, and reached Montreal in May of 1910. Leaving Montreal by train for Detroit, Franjo thought it would be easier for him to enter the United States at the Canadian/American border, but this proved not to be the case. Once again, Franjo was denied entrance by the inspectors due to the diagnosis of trachoma and was sent back to Canada for further eye treatment. After Canadian doctors told Franjo that his eyes were okay and only showed signs of scar tissues, he was even more determined to complete his immigration. However, the story of his final step of immigration has two conflicting stories about his American border crossing. The result would be the same.

The outcome of Franjo's immigration would be an indication of what would come to be in the next century, as immigrants today want to desperately share in the freedom and prosperity of the American people. Franjo's future descendants and most citizens today take for granted their American citizenship; but we all should keep in mind what a future of being in America means to people trying to immigrate into our country whether from the eastern and southern areas of Europe or from Mexico and Central America. The reality for them is one worth cost, struggle, danger, and even death for people wanting a better life.

Franjo Palaich's immigration story had always been told to my father, Frank, and to all Franjo's grandchildren and is a narrative that has always been consistent. When Franjo was sent back to Windsor at the Canadian/American border, he was even more determined that this would be his final attempt to become an American. The Detroit River that separates the two countries is one to one-half miles across, which Franjo knew he could be easily swim. Grandpa's final attempt into entering the United States would be to swim across the Detroit River from Windsor, Canada. Hard work, determination, love of America would be the stimulus that would drive him to endanger himself and what he believed in for the rest of his life.

Years later, after Franjo's death, a letter was found in the basement within old papers of our grandmother.

It was written sometime after 1930 to the Immigration or Naturalization Department of the United States, but before Franjo's death in 1954, and most of the letter reiterated Franjo's immigration story that had always been part of family history. The final step in the letter tells of an entirely different ending to his immigration story. After being denied entrance at the Detroit US border crossing, Franjo wrote to the US Immigration or Naturalization Office the following:

> *...this time, I went across Niagara Falls Bridge in this way avoided going through another examination. After two years, I got married and now have three children, two girls and a boy. I am very thankful, dear American citizens all these years I was living here in Detroit, worried, trying, asking about any possible way to become a citizen of US. Nobody could advise me, so I decided to bring out everything that had happened and find out if there is any possible way, I could become an American citizen. I will be thankful in every way to become a citizen of US so I can say I am an American citizen, which I've wanted to be for so many years.*

It is not known if the letter was ever mailed, but what is known regrettably, is Franjo never achieved his desire of becoming an American citizen. Also, it is believed that because he was an illegal alien or never wanted to be denied entry into his beloved and adopted new country, he never left the Detroit area in the 44 years he lived in the US. He never returned to his family in Croatia.

For over 44 years, my grandfather modeled the traits of a successful man, which wasn't easy for an Eastern European to have at that time in our nation's history. Detroit at the time of Franjo's immigration was made up of Anglo-Saxon Protestants and some Irish Catholics. Only after 1910 did most other European nationalities emigrate to the United States. They left their countries due to religious, political, and economic hardship. The prejudice towards these "foreigners" made success stories of non-English speaking Catholic immigrants harder to achieve; much like the experience

Franjo Palaich *as a young man in Detroit in 1915 at age 28.*

of the current influx of foreign-born in America today. Franjo would use his butcher trade to support his family and proceeded to do so with hard work and the determination that allowed him to be in America in the first place. Despite his worries of being an illegal alien, Franjo opened his first grocery store and butcher shop on Riopelle St. and opened another market on Hull St. His success story continued by being one of the first of his group of Croatians to own a home while others rented. In 1940, he was able to buy a cottage in Lake Orion within a watery area of Metro Detroit named Bunny Run, as well as a flat in Detroit. He shared the lower flat with family members and used the upper flat as rental property.

By his loving example and his mantra of "work hard and honest work," our grandfather taught us early his way of life. We saw him as a serious, quiet, hardworking man respected by all who knew him. He showed us by example how to care for those around us and to share with others what we were fortunate to have. During the Depression, he would give store credit to those in his neighborhood to purchase food, never asking or expecting repayment. Years after his death, old customer-owned bills were found buried in family records. His cottage in Bunny Run was opened to family and friends for summer enjoyment to share Croatian recipes and customs, keeping up with cultural ideals and changes.

Today, the only people who can remember Franjo are his grandchildren, who are now older grandparents themselves, and the memories we have of him are old but warm and loving. We now know that through grandpa's hard work and sacrifice as an immigrant, he brought to us advantages and knowledge of achieving the American dream as well as a strong sense of values that included righteousness, kindness, and love of family and country. We know through him that our person is measured by the quality of our actions, meant to be honest, sincere, and generous, despite prejudice and hatred towards immigrants and the awareness of the hardships that these actions can bring. I pray that the younger descendants of Franjo obtain these same qualities, and that they see through prejudice and hatred, that they make changes for immigrants wanting the same advantages, while accepting challenges that immigrants had in earlier years of American history.

When Franjo landed at Ellis Island, he was aware of the plaque at the base of the Statue of Liberty that reads: "Give me your tired, your poor, your huddled masses yearning to breathe free, the wretched refuse of your teeming shore. Send these, the homeless, tempest-tossed to me, I lift my lamp beside the golden door!"

All Franjo's success came to him because he could live in this welcoming nation. In peace, free from political harassment, he worked hard with strong moral values, determined not to let other people with prejudice and hatred lower his ideals or determination. Sadly, this is not the case in United States today. Illegal aliens are no longer allowed peace. They experience fear and trauma in their lives as they ache for better opportunities to feed their families and to have a higher quality of life than in their country of origin. The golden door that once welcomed even illegal aliens is closing in.

Nahid Rachlin *went to the Columbia University Writing Program on a Doubleday-Columbia Fellowship and then went on to Stanford University writing program on a Wallace Stegner Fellowship. Her publications include a memoir,* Persian Girls *(Penguin), four novels, including* Foreigner *(W.W. Norton),* Married to a Stranger *(E.P.Dutton-Penguin) and a short story collection,* Veils *(City Lights). For more click on:* http://www. nahidrachlin.com/index.htm

Nahid Rachlin

I GREW UP in Tehran and Ahvaz, two cities in Iran. I was one among seven siblings, two brothers and four sisters in a Muslim family. My father, though highly educated, a lawyer, still believed that education was for his sons and that his daughters' paths after high school should be marriage.

I rebelled against that role and expressed my dissatisfaction in writing, trying to give shape to what seemed chaotic and incomprehensible to me. After doing my schoolwork I spent a few hours writing short stories. When I approached the end of high school, still rebelling against any prescribed role, and wanting to pursue higher education and my writing, I argued with my father to send me to college in the United States, where my two brothers were by then. Finally, my father gave in, mostly because he was afraid what I wrote would get me and the family into trouble. In the 1960s, under the Shah's regime, there was heavy censorship of books and of any spoken word that could be interpreted as criticism of the culture or government. My father gave in to my pressure, but under the condition of attending a college near one of my brothers, so that he could look after me. I was accepted to an all-women college with a full scholarship and that cemented my way for immigrating to the US. But getting adjusted to the college was a struggle, though ultimately it gave me the freedom to pursue my goal of becoming a writer.

Beauty contests and mixers with boys that the school invited from colleges in the area just floated around me without meaning. The ideal young girl, one whom the staff and parents approved of and promoted, always dressed properly, was agreeable and sociable. If a student didn't go on frequent dates with boys, she was "anti-social," or a "loser." If most students had plans with a female friend, and then a boy called and asked her out at the same time, they would automatically accept the date and cancel plans with the girlfriend. Smiling for females was compulsory. One girl in my dormitory said, "Smile" every time we passed each other in the hall.

The pocket money Father sent me through my brother shrunk when converted from toomans to dollars. The other girls flew home often for family gatherings or to reunite with a high school sweetheart. They had their hair done in expensive beauty salons in St. Louis, then went shopping and returned with packages of hats, gloves, blouses, shoes. They often skipped dormitory meals to buy their own food. The girls who didn't have cars took taxis everywhere rather than buses, which ran infrequently on limited routes. They decorated their rooms with their own personal furniture. I was out of the prison of my home but then I was here all alone. I didn't know a single person other than my brother, who was busy with his own studies as a medical student.

One day, towards the end of the semester, I found a note from the dean in my mailbox. She invited me, along with the other three foreign students on the campus, to participate in Parents' Day, and asked that I stop by her office. The dean wore a linen suit, her blond hair set in neat short curls; she greeted me with a warm smile.

"I'm telling this to all the foreign students on the campus," she said. "That you should wear your native costumes on Parents' Day." I was silent, feeling awkward. I had no costume. She was waiting.

"In Iran, some women cover themselves in chadors, but they wear them on top of regular clothes, similar to what people wear here," I said.

"Then wear a chador," she said.

My awkwardness only increased.

"I never wore one in Iran," I said finally, my voice drowning in the sound of laughter and conversations in the hall.

"I still want you to wear it for this occasion, to show a little of your culture to us," she said, smiling cheerfully.

To me the chador had come to mean a kind of bondage. It felt ridiculous to wear it in this American college. "Maybe I can think of something else to wear," I mumbled.

"No, no, the idea of the chador is excellent. I've seen pictures of women in the Islamic countries wearing them. It fascinates me. What is the point?"

"Well in Islam, exposed hair and skin is considered to be seductive to men."

"I wish I could feel my hair and skin are so seductive that I'd have to cover them up," she said with a chuckle. But her attempt at humor only made me more insecure in this unexpectedly alien environment.

As I trudged through my days in a place where I didn't fit, I tried to focus on my future. I would go somewhere in America where I could blend in more, though I had no idea yet where that was or how I would get there.

I reminded myself of the luxury of being able to read and write what I wanted without Father's vigilant eyes on me, or the fear in my heart of SAVAK, the Shah's secret police. Late at night I turned to my writing, my long-lasting friend. I wrote in English now, though I had to constantly look up words in a dictionary. Even though no one was watching me, fear of discovery still attacked me at times, as if Father or a SAVAK agent were lurking in the dark. Writing in English gave me a feeling of freedom I didn't feel in Farsi.

I continued with my writing as I received fellowships in MFA programs at Columbia University and Stanford University. My first published novel, *Foreigner*, expresses the division an immigrant feels, missing aspects of home and not quite feeling like an American, and the loneliness that goes with it.

Joneil "Juni" Robinson *lives in Orlando, Florida where she enjoys the rainy and sunny days. She graduated Summa Cum Laude from the University of Central Florida. She is working as a personal assistant to a surgeon. She loves studying birds, illustration and watching forensic science documentaries in her spare time.*

Joneil "Juni" Robinson

FOR SOMEONE who has been living in the United States for most of her life, I do feel a great sense of pride in knowing that I'm from Canada. I was born in Scarborough, a tiny suburb within Toronto, Ontario. When I share my origin, I typically receive a reaction of puzzlement and interest. From various remarks like never meeting a Black Canuck, if I spoke fluent French, to being asked about my love for the violent sport of hockey (which is true), my identity as a Canadian is one often unexpected.

Because I was young when I emigrated to America, the date of my arrival isn't something I have knowledge of. Based on what my parents have shared, I arrived when I was three years old. Before the future would bring me two more siblings, I was accompanied just by my mother and father who also happened to be immigrants but instead from Jamaica, not Canada.

The decision to move from Canada to the United States was something I didn't have any say in since I was just a little child. My mother had many siblings that had moved to the United States. The main reason for leaving still strikes me to this day. My mother was the only one in our small, immediate family that absolutely hated the cold. My father was, and still is, an enthusiast of cold climates, which I, too, developed a liking for. But since my mother disliked the frigidity of what Canada can offer, it was a shared decision to leave and to move all the way to the southern peninsula we know as Florida.

Getting used to being on American soil wasn't particularly difficult since we didn't have to worry about language barriers but moving to Okeechobee was a struggle in itself based on the cultural divide in the town. As Black immigrants in a rural area, our identities were often the target of discrimination and racial prejudice, something completely out of our control. I had a preschool teacher that would exclaim how much trouble I would cause and would single me out in my predominantly Caucasian class. My father was asked by a cashier about using WIC (Special Supplemental Nutrition Program for Women, Infants, and Children) when buying groceries, which other white customers before him weren't asked. My father didn't even have a clue what WIC was until he shared the odd inquiry with my mother, who was livid with the idea that they would assume such a thing about us based off of what we looked like.

But despite dealing with bouts of racial prejudice, I experienced plenty of success as an immigrant in America. I was able to soon receive my US citizenship and made many friends throughout grade school. I graduated from high school and soon went to my local community college to receive an associate degree before transferring to the University of Central Florida. I've had these jobs: caretaker, case manager, administrative assistant, teaching assistant, camp counselor, and a technician at a hospital in Florida. My career has had its ups and downs as many service industry jobs do, but for each position I've obtained I've been continuously praised for my work ethic, optimistic personality and desire to always go above what is expected of me.

Although moving to a country with different cultures and ideals was a shock at first for my family and me, living here in America is something I enjoy! The friends, family and wonderful experiences I've gained while growing up on this soil are aspects of my life that would have not come about had I been in another place. Being different can make you stick out like a sore thumb sometimes, but I wouldn't change my heritage for a thing.

Louis Roose

I MARRIED BERTHA on April 1, 1925. The next day my wife and I left Belgium, hoping to reach the United States via Canada. We had decided to go south and set out for the "Land of Opportunity." We wanted to live in Detroit. We took a rowboat and crossed the Detroit River in the dark of night.

I grew up on a farm in Belgium. We were five boys and five girls. Were the farm to be divided, each sibling would have a very small parcel. At that time families frequently had bars serving beer and wine in front of their homes. That's how I met Bertha. Her family owned the establishment Stadt Torhout and I left the bar not only with a beer but with a Bertha.

There were some 80 Germans who lived in in our home during World War I. A German soldier had lifted his rifle and motioned to Bertha that he was going to shoot the enemy the next day. Then, by mistake, he shot off her ear. She was devastated, but she forgave him.

On May 14, 1976, local historian Don Baut interviewed Bertha and me about our emigration to the United States. I explained that upon reaching Canada, we immediately proceeded to Windsor's Assumption College where a priest offered me a job. I worked at a greenhouse in LaSalle.

During those days, it was not easy to leave our country and go to America. We had to wait for long periods of time. But to immigrate to Canada was easy. In 1958 my wife and I returned to Antwerp to get our papers in order and to visit the World's Fair that was held in Belgium the same year.

Louis Roose *passed away playing golf with his son Ed on the golf course in 1994. This article is based on an interview conducted by the Dearborn Historical Museum for its archives.*

My first job in the US was to work as a roofer. I fell off the roof on my first day and broke my leg. I then worked in the concrete business and at a slaughterhouse. My brother-in-law was a janitor at Annunciation Parish in Detroit. The pastor and Fr. Alphonse X. Sharpe at Dearborn's Sacred Heart were friends, and the Annunciation pastor said he wanted a Belgian janitor. My interview went well. Bertha said it was because Belgians were good workers. I worked at Sacred Heart for 38 years. There was no church when I began working there in 1928. Church services were held in the school.

It was a different era when I worked at Sacred Heart. My son told me that everyone would know where I was working in the school as my cigar smoke would fill the area. The nuns loved how I was thorough and quick at cleaning. They begged me rather than my assistant to clean their classrooms.

For three years, we lived above the pastor's garage where our first son, Maurice, was born. In 1941, we moved to a Ford Home, a Model E, at 22744 Nona. I was frugal. I saved every penny to make a $3400 down payment to purchase the home. My monthly house payment was $34. I made it my mission to pay off my loan early. The family that held the mortgage bemoaned the fact that they would no longer be receiving interest! We referred to our enclosed porch as "the cottage" and would sit on it each evening after going for a walk.

At Mass one Sunday, Bertha noted that the woman sitting next to her had a Flemish prayer book. They immediately took a liking into each other. The Belgian woman was Maria DeCaluwe, whose husband was the head gardener at Fair Lane, Henry Ford's estate. The DeCaluwe family lived in one of the three cottages on the grounds. Ultimately, they would move to the gate house From then on, we spent time together as couples. Alfons DeCaluwe and I played two-handed pinochle each Friday night. I would be so immersed in the game that my son Ed recalls drinking the remainder of my beer when he was a toddler.

As a result of this friendship with the DeCaluwes, we would frequently see the auto magnate and his family. One day Mr. Ford asked my daughter Helen if she wanted to go for a bike ride. When she said that she didn't have a bike, Mr. Ford bought her one. Helen went on to spend 19 years in the convent of the Sister Servants of the Immaculate Heart of Mary.

Domestic life was not easy. On one occasion Bertha broke a chair over Maurice's head as the two were discussing his wedding plans. We had had one child who was stillborn and another who died of pneumonia at the age of nine months.

When I retired, I had no pension. However, after I had left my employment, the pastor at Sacred Heart called to tell me that the Archdiocese of Detroit had created a pension program and if I returned to work for a year, I would be eligible for retirement benefits. I returned to Sacred Heart so that I could receive a $138 monthly pension.

I loved playing par three golf. Dying on the golf course would not be a bad way to go.

George Smith

I WAS BORN in Manchester, England. My dad was a bus driver. When I was growing up, classism was rampant. My parents owned neither a car nor a home. In England you couldn't borrow money for these basics unless you had a certain level of income, which my parents didn't have. I expected that I would have the same fortune. I remember only having ridden in a car twice by the time I immigrated with my parents to Canada when I was sixteen.

I never cared for the classroom. I was always bored and getting into trouble. My dad encouraged me to leave school when I was fifteen. I did and ended up with an apprenticeship as a toolmaker. I was thrilled. That changed my whole life.

The Canadian authorities wanted to expand their economy from one based primarily on the exploitation of natural resources to one that had a dynamic business sector. They needed more people to make this happen. At that time, the Canadian government was putting out the welcome mat for immigrants from English speaking countries.

I suspect that my parents' reason for coming to Canada was primarily economic. There simply were more opportunities in Canada than in the United Kingdom. A lot of my parents' friends came to Canada. I came with my parents by boat in 1954.

While my dad had driven a bus for 30 years in England, he could not find a job in our new country for four months. I found a job with the Firestone Tire and Rubber Company in Hamilton, Ontario. Ultimately,

George Smith *lives with his wife Marge in Livonia, Michigan. They have been happily married for 21 years. George loves helping others and serving the Lord. He also loves reading books and watching documentaries.*

I got my dad a job with the same company. I did not have trouble adapting to life in North America. However, after my dad had driven a bus for so long in England, he had a difficult time adjusting to driving on the right side of the road.

I couldn't believe my good fortune. I bought a 1938 four-door Dodge sedan. I paid $75 for it, and the day I purchased it, I forgot about England.

I lived in Canada for 18 years before moving to the United States. I worked in purchasing. In 1973 I was transferred to Virginia.

I was always eager to learn and hungry to stay busy. I worked my way up the ladder in the automotive industry. I can honestly say that I became a "captain of industry." I became the global purchasing director for one of my employers. I loved every day of my working life. I always was in high pressure jobs and was rewarded handsomely. I worked for 53 years and never had a bad day. At the end of my career I had 3500 people reporting to me. I say with humility that I was able to increase morale and attendance among my subordinates.

While success in my career was important, I think that my membership in my church was the most important part of my life. For 14 years, I have belonged to the Full Gospel Temple Church in Westland, Michigan. It impacted my life. I enjoy serving the Lord and helping others.

I was married three times. I had four sons and one daughter. In 1999, I married the love of my life, Marjorie.

My children were from my first two marriages. Grant, James, and Matthew were from my first marriage. Stephen and Sarah were from my second marriage. My children achieved levels in North America that they would not have achieved in England.

My son, Grant, was valedictorian in high school, and he was always top salesman both in the men's clothing business and automotive sales. Unfortunately, Grant was diagnosed with cancer and the Lord took him home in 2015.

James did very well in school and is an information technology expert. He recently started a new business with two other partners. I am certain they will do well.

Matthew also did well in school and started his own business which was very successful.

Stephen was my first child to go to college and get a business degree. He served in the US Army for ten years. He served four of those years in Baghdad. He served as an "advance man" for President Obama for two years in the White House. He is now serving as a civilian employee for the US Department of Defense in Germany.

Sarah was valedictorian in high school and class president. She was offered an academic scholarship from Florida State University but always wanted to go to the University of Virginia. She has been in the arts and entertainment industry since she graduated in 2004. She lives in Los Angeles.

I love the United States. I live a very good life. As a young man, I never thought I would own my own home. Today, I live in a nice home. I also paid for the homes of my former two wives. I supported my mother for 13 years while she was in a nursing home. Where else could someone who was as uneducated as I have been so successful?

I am blessed with a good wife, Marjorie. Who could ask for anything more?

Marina Terterian

I AM ARMENIAN by nationality, and a naturalized American citizen. My journey to America began 28 years ago on September 18, 1991 when my sister, Inna Muradyan, and I flew aboard a Pan American flight that landed in Detroit late at night.

The actual journey began two years earlier when my family and hundreds of thousands of Armenians were trapped in the middle of an ethnic conflict between two republics of the former Soviet Union: Armenia and Azerbaijan and a region called Nagorno Karabakh (Artsakh).

I was born and raised in Baku, the capital of Azerbaijan, a republic of the former Soviet Union. I lived in the multicultural, multinational city among many other nationalities who co-existed and worked together. I was living a very comfortable life. I earned my master's degree in engineering in 1982 and worked at the Institute of Cybernetics at the Academy of Science. Three years later, I worked on my "Patent Expert Diploma" through the Correspondence Institute in Moscow. Nothing foreshadowed the dark days that were to come. Violence, attacks, pogroms, fear, desperation, casualties and clashes between Armenians (Christians) and Azerbaijanis (Muslims) who ruled during that era. No one could imagine and predict that our lives would abruptly change by early 1988.

In the 1920s, the Soviet government established the Nagorno-Karabakh Autonomous Region—where 95 percent of the population was ethnically Armenian—within the territory of Azerbaijan. Under Bolshevik rule,

Marina Terterian *lives in Rochester Hills, Michigan. She enjoys her summer break from teaching by visiting the Farmers Market on weekends, making the preserves from locally grown fruits and walking on the National Paint Creek Trail in the area.*

fighting between the two countries was kept in check, but as the Soviet Union began to collapse, so did its grip on Armenia and Azerbaijan. In 1988, the Nagorno-Karabakh legislature passed a resolution to join Armenia despite the region's legal location within Azerbaijan's borders. Ethnic conflict began after the declaration of independence. War erupted between Armenia and Azerbaijan over the region, leaving roughly 30,000 casualties and hundreds of thousands of refugees.

Two hundred and fifty thousand Armenians who were living in Baku, the capital of Azerbaijan, had to flee or face being beaten or murdered. People became refugees overnight. One day they were living peacefully in their own country and the next, they lost everything and were forced to leave their homes. It was an indescribably devastating feeling of emptiness and shock. Beyond the imagination, a nightmare.

The United States of America immediately acknowledged the situation as an ordeal, and it granted us refugee status. It was comforting to know we would be safe. America became my country, the country where I could find peace, make a home, and build a family.

My sister and I arrived in Detroit, Michigan with two suitcases and two hundred dollars in our pocket to begin our new lives. The realization that we needed to start over came to us a bit later. It is said that "Rome was not built in a day." To restart our lives again was not easy. But after slowly adjusting to a new life and new culture, meeting new people, and being introduced to the local Armenian community, I became acclimated to my new country. I realized I was given the opportunity to immigrate and I was given the opportunity not only to survive but to succeed. I was given the chance to build my own life and to be content. We were sponsored by the Catholic Archdiocese of Detroit, which helped us with our needs. We were then able to save some money, buy our first car, and move to Ann Arbor, Michigan.

My first job was as a cataloging assistant for the Slavic Department Graduate Library at the University of Michigan. Most people I worked with were scholars and immigrants themselves. Working in such a diverse department made me realize how big this country is.

We shared our stories at potluck dinners. Years have passed, and now I have a beautiful family: my husband, Kazar Terterian; my daughter, Ani; and son, Tigran. Both my children are pursuing higher education, which is key to success. I found my passion in teaching, and I have been teaching mathematics and physical science courses at community colleges for almost twenty years. Throughout my teaching career, I have encouraged my students to not give up quickly, but to build self-confidence and to work hard towards their goals. I explain that hard work will always be rewarded and that their success lies is in their own hands. Everyone can succeed and success should be treasured.

CPSIA information can be obtained
at www.ICGtesting.com
Printed in the USA
BVHW020710021020
589700BV00005B/2